M000221852

A native of Derry, David Dickson is a Senior Lecturer in the Department of Modern History, Trinity College Dublin. He has written extensively on the social and political evolution of eighteenth and early nineteenth century Ireland and has a particular interest in regional history. He is currently Co-Director of the National Famine Research Project, a government funded investigation of the Great Famine of 1845-51.

ARCTIC IRELAND

David Dickson

The White Row Press

ARCTIC IRELAND

David Dickson

The White Row Press

First published 1997, Reprinted 1998
by the White Row Press Ltd.
135 Cumberland Road, Dundonald
Belfast BT16 0BB

Copyright © David Dickson
All rights reserved

This book has received financial assistance
under the Cultural Traditions Programme

Cover: Dunbar Design
Cover & text illustration: Geoffrey Fulton

Typesetting: Island Publications
Printed by the Guernsey Press Company Limited

A catalogue record for this book is available from the British Library

ISBN 1 870132 85 8

Contents

Preface

This book seeks to offer a brief narrative account of two extraordinary years in Irish social history. The events of 1740 and 1741 have long passed from public knowledge and usually merit no more than a line or two in summary histories of Ireland. Thirty years ago Michael Drake was the first modern scholar to draw attention to the crisis and its significance, and since then the writings of John Post and Louis Cullen have greatly helped to put the Irish catastrophe into context. There is an obvious debt to the three of them in what follows. I am also very grateful to my publisher, Peter Carr, for his initial encouragement and inspired direction of a wayward author.

I would like to thank the following for permission to quote from manuscript collections in their care: the Council of Trustees of the National Library of Ireland, the Public Record Office of Northern Ireland, the British Library, the National Library of Wales, and the Armagh Public Library. Financial support for some of the research on which this book is based came from the Arts Benefaction Fund in Trinity College Dublin.

D.D.
Dublin
August 1997

1
The big freeze

It may all have started a year previously and on the other side of the world: great volcanic eruptions on the remote Kamchatka peninsula, pumping thousands of tons of dust into the upper atmosphere, may have been sufficient to upset the meteorological equilibrium of the northern hemisphere. Or perhaps it was triggered by no more than the random flight of an Amazonian butterfly. No definitive scientific explanation for the extraordinary climatic shocks that hit Europe between December 1739 and September 1741 has as yet been advanced.

In Ireland these twenty-one months of bizarre weather were without known precedent and defied conventional explanation. On the eve of the crisis there had perhaps been some complacency as to the power of exceptional weather to upset normal life. Winters had been relatively benign over the previous thirty years. No one, not even those with distant memories of the terrible winters of the 1680s, was prepared for what became known as the Great Frost of 1740, or for *bliain an áir*, the year of slaughter, of 1741. Indeed, the time of the Great Frost remains to this day the longest period of extreme cold in modern European history.

Scientific enthusiasts in Dublin and Cork had begun to measure weather, specifically rainfall and temperature, but they could offer little insight into why 'the most violent storm... for several years past', roaring in from the east on the 29th and 30th December 1739, introduced a cold so penetrating that

The body was found 'covered over with ice'.

liquids froze indoors and ice floes appeared at the river mouths. Nor would they account for the subsequent extremes of wind, drought or recurring cold that were to be visited on the country in the course of the twenty-one months to come.

No barometric or temperature readings for Ireland made during the Great Frost survive. A reliable mercury thermometer had been developed by the Dutch pioneer Fahrenheit twenty-five years before, but even in England there were only a few men who by 1739 were in the habit of regularly taking temperature readings. Startling indoor values were noted there during January 1740, ranging as low as 10°F; the one outdoor English reading was of a temperature close to thirty-two degrees of frost. Such truly Arctic cold, compounded as it initially was by a severe wind-chill factor, was quite outside British or Irish experience. In Scotland, an Edinburgh writer referred to the terrible January wind as 'piercing Nova Zembla air'.[1] A Cork priest-poet writing in Irish spoke of:

> A northern cross which hit the Irish people,
> A hard shower of frost which was driven out of Styx...

and of the biting winds, which heralded a time of sorrow, pain, debt and hardship.[2]

There was New Year mayhem around the Irish coast. Three

vessels were lost in Dublin Bay – an incoming French ship laded with brandy, a Riga fly-boat with flaxseed, and a Liverpool sloop with salt, earthenware and passengers; all the latter were drowned, the body of the sloop's master being found on Merrion Strand 'covered over with ice'.[3]

The winds lasted for less than a week, but the terrible cold intensified in the course of January 1740. Yet hardly any snow fell. Ireland was locked into a stable and vast high-pressure system which affected most of Europe, from Scandinavia and Russia to northern Italy, in a broadly similar way. The most visible immediate consequence in Ireland was the transformation of the rivers and lakes: the Liffey, the Slaney, the Boyne, the Foyle, and sections of the Shannon were reported frozen within days, as were Loughs Cong and Neagh. In England there were reports of a total freeze-up on Windermere, the Norfolk Broads, and the Tyne, of 'the silver Thames' being bound 'in icy chains', and of monumental icicles where waterfalls had been held in

Many revelled in the novelty of their new climate. Carnivals and banquets were held on the ice.

their tracks. Fish were the earliest recorded victims: in the first weeks of the Frost vast quantities were found dead around the shores of Strangford Lough and Lough Neagh.[4]

Some people were simply delighted by the novelty of it all. What were in effect carnivals or banquets on ice were held at many venues across Ireland. The Dublin press carried numerous reports of such events in the early weeks of the Frost; a municipal sheep-roasting took place on the Boyne at Navan where the local gentlemen and their wives performed 'several country dances on the ice, being attended by a large band of music';[5] north Tipperary gentry roasted a whole sheep on top of nineteen inches of Shannon ice near Portumna, 'at the eating of which they had great mirth, and drank many loyal toasts'; afterwards 'a match of hurling' was played between two gentlemen's teams. Extravaganzas took place in Britain – a frost fair on the Thames, a great sheep roasting on the Tyne, a women's curling match on the Nithdale ice near Dumfries, occasions redolent of the great seventeenth-century Dutch depictions of sociability on ice.[6]

Others used the frozen lakes as welcome shortcuts. Folk were walking from the Tyrone shore of Lough Neagh over ten miles of ice to Antrim market in mid-January. Some travellers were however caught on treacherous sections of ice; disaster hit a funeral cortege on Lough Cong in County Galway, and six were drowned trying to cross the frozen Foyle outside Derry.[7]

The all-pervasive cold had immediate effects on everyday life. Most obviously there was the problem of how to stave off catastrophic hypothermia and preserve minimal body warmth without using up all one's reserves of winter fuel in a matter of days. Country people rarely traded turf in winter-time, and certainly not in January 1740. The task of staying minimally warm may been easier in country cabins that lay abreast of reassuring turf stacks than in the freezing basements and garret dwellings of poorer families in the towns. Urban dwellers in the east- and south-coast ports were in normal times dependent on a shuttle service of small boats bringing coal from Cumbria and south Wales. Now, however, ice-bound quays and frozen coal

Hedges, 'fine trees', and nurseries were stripped bare in the desperate search for fuel.

yards brought the trade to an abrupt standstill. When in late January the traffic across the Irish Sea resumed, the retail price of coal soared so that many households simply could not afford it. Hedges, 'fine trees', and nurseries around Dublin were being stripped bare as desperate people searched for substitute fuel. Fourteen were arrested for tree-felling in the Phoenix Park; 'fair dealing from [the] colliers might have prevented a great deal of this mischief', remarked one city printer.[8] The coal dealers and shippers were seen as the authors of this mischief, and in London similar animosity was being directed against the 'villainous' Tyneside coalmen.

Then there was the Frost's effects on the wider economy. Pre-industrial towns depended on the constant activity of dozens of mill-wheels. Water powered the machinery which ground wheat for the bakers, tucked cloth for the weavers, pulped rags for the printers. But now the mills were paralyzed, and both craft employment and food processing were completely disrupted. The Frost also plunged the streets of Dublin into darkness at night, for not only were there problems in milling the rape-seed to make the customary lamp-oil, but even fully serviced lamps were being snuffed out by the intense cold.[9]

2

Alms and gestures: early rescue operations

Natural calamity tests the administrative structures and social bonds of any society. Ireland in 1740 was by contemporary western European standards lightly governed, materially poor, and socially polarized. Its governing class, an overwhelmingly Protestant landed gentry, had inherited from the seventeenth century an essentially negative view of the rural majority: the latter were treated with suspicion on account of their Catholicism, their supposed disloyalty towards the Hanoverian state, and their apparent lack of enthusiasm for the kinds of improved farming that promised to raise the future value of landed property.

However the gentry and the merchants who were in charge of municipal government displayed more positive attitudes towards artisans and tradespeople, urban and rural. They took far greater notice when these people were in trouble than when small farmers alone were in distress. In part this disparity of concern was self-interested – artisans and petty entrepreneurs were the sinews of the commercial economy on which the owners of broad acres depended. In part it reflected the importance the propertied classes attached to the maintenance of order, urban discontent being regarded as a more immediate and potent threat than anything that might happen in the countryside. And, furthermore, an unemployed or hungry town often became a sickly town and such sickness might be no respecter of class or wealth. The attitudes of the dominant elite were also coloured by religion: there was a markedly higher proportion of Protestants among tradespeople and artisans than among the farming classes at large.

The early response by the propertied classes was therefore primarily an urban one; this may indeed have been justified by the greater vulnerability of townsfolk to fuel and food shortages, and to the loss of gainful employment. When the crisis was about a fortnight old, charity collections began in Dublin for the multitude of weavers who were unable to work, and for other poorer households in the city. Newspaper appeals were used to drum up donations, and these were channelled towards the Church of Ireland parish clergy or to the formal parish officers and vestries of the Established Church, which at that stage were the lowest tier of local government in the larger towns.

In the capital, money was raised quite quickly, mainly in the wealthier eastern parishes where a number of resident aristocrats and parliament men lent their names to vigorous fund-raising. These donations were then converted into free rations in the western city parishes: nearly eighty tons of coal and ten tons of meal were distributed in the fourth week of the Frost, by which time it was reported there were 'many thousand [sic] starving'. In keeping with the minimalist concepts of what then constituted the civil responsibilities of government, the Lord Lieutenant, the Duke of Devonshire, did not attempt to coordinate a national response to the emergency. He contributed £100 from the public purse to the city appeal in Dublin, and in response to a request from Cork Corporation he authorized a proclamation on the 19th January prohibiting the export of grain out of the kingdom to any destination bar Britain. This was an unprecedented move.[10] But it was about the sum total of government-directed action for eleven months.

Across the country in the weeks of the Great Frost three types of relief agency were evident. There were the Church of Ireland parish authorities (the minister or his vestry) who ran the local 'dole' committees which received the *douceurs* of the wealthy, including the contributions from absentee landowners, and organized distributions in cash or in kind; this parochial activity was an expansion of a normal alms-giving service which in better times was restricted to the old and infirm, usually members of the congregation. Where Protestant numbers were particularly thin on the ground such parish committees probably did not materialize. In the small Presbyterian world of Belfast, 'the reverend ministers of the four congregations' plus three laymen from each congregation established a charitable committee which in late January organized a house-to-house alms collection, and distributed the monies raised (approximately £150) to some 850 distressed towns-people.[11]

Secondly, there were those town authorities who decided to intervene in the food markets to try and control prices and to prevent trouble down the line. Cork Corporation was notably quick to engage in bulk grain and meal purchasing in mid-January with the intention of selling it at subsidized rates in public markets; there was a lively memory in the city of events eleven years before when serious food riots had ended up with four people dead.[12]

Thirdly, there was the direct response of landowners and employers to evidence of suffering among their tenants and dependants; very little is recorded of what resident landlords may or may not have done, but the decisions of non-residents to authorize their agents to distribute specific sums were regularly mentioned in the newspapers. Lady Brownlow of Waringstown, County Armagh, gave directions from France that £440 should distributed 'among such of her poor tenants as have suffered in the late rigorous season'; and John Damer was reported to have given over £1,500 to the poor 'of all denominations' in County

Tipperary, 'some in ready money, the rest in corn'; this (if true) was probably the largest act of generosity in 1740.   It was not just the powerful and the wealthy who provided financial help; there was for example the case of Mrs Jamisson, owner of a hosiery business in the Dublin Cornmarket, who carried her gang of journeymen through the crisis by giving them cash advances.[13]

Ireland was in the grip of the Frost for nearly seven weeks – not as bad as Paris where there were seventy-five days of continuous frost, or of Uppsala in Sweden where sub-zero temperatures continued for fourteen weeks.   On the 3rd of February Dean Swift hoped that 'we have almost done with this cursed weather...', and the Irish papers reported some relief from the iron Frost in the second week of February; the Liffey was no longer safe for a promenade.[14]   A thaw was coming.

3
'The most dreadful calamity': the annihilation of the potato

The Siberian winter was the first of a series of strange seasons. But even if entirely normal weather patterns had resumed in March 1740 the after-effects of such a winter would have long persisted.   This was principally because the Great Frost had played havoc with one of the two main sources of food in rural Ireland – the potato.   In many districts 'the Irish root' was at least as important as oatmeal in everyday nutrition.   But this was not to be the case in 1740.   As early as New Year's Day Michael Rivers, a Dungarvan, County Waterford merchant, told his Dublin correspondent how it was said that the frost:

> has already destroyed a great part of the potatoes that
> lie in the cabins that lodge them and most of the

The potatoes had turned into formless mush.

potatoes of our country that are in ground, by which the poor are likely to suffer greatly...[15]

An even more pessimistic assessment was made by Richard Purcell, a north Cork estate agent, three weeks later:

The eating potatoes are all destroyed, which many think will be followed by a famine among the poor, and if the small ones, which are not bigger than large peas and which be deepest in the ground, are so destroyed as not to serve for seed, there must be a sore famine in 1741... if no potatoes remain sound for seed, I think this frost the most dreadful calamity that ever befell this poor kingdom.[16]

Tens of thousands of small-farming and labouring families, as they shivered in their cabins across the country, had to come to terms with the sudden loss of their principal winter foodstuff.[17] The ripened potatoes, left in apparent security in gardens and fields where they had grown, had now been rendered quite inedible as a direct result of being frozen.

A run of relatively mild winters during the previous decade had perhaps lulled people into a sense of false security as regards their food supply. Indeed in Lord Chancellor's Jocelyn's view this was one of the causes of the crisis: 'the lower sort... being used to soft seasons for many years, have neglected to lay up a sufficient provision, either for their families or cattle'. During that time the relative importance of the potato in the diet of the rural poor had continued to grow. Other foodstuffs of course remained popular in winter and spring – notably milk and cabbage. But while the consumption of meal (whether in the form of porridge or of coarse unleavened bread) was still fundamentally important in the diet of even the very poor, its use was mainly from May until potato-digging time in late summer. The strategic importance of the potato as the main foodstuff was greatest in the south, in the Munster dairying, sheep-ranching and cattle-fattening communities. Indeed a number of coastal districts in the south of the province had pioneered the commercial production of potatoes, mainly for consumption in Dublin and Cork.[18]

Richard Purcell, one of the best rural witnesses of the unfolding crisis, reported in late February that had the Frost not occurred, there would have been enough potatoes in his district to have kept the country fed until August, indicating a rare local abundance of the crop. 'But both root and branch... is destroyed every where', except for 'a few which happen'd to be housed', and 'in a very few deep... and turfy moulded gardens where some, perhaps enough for seed for the same ground, are sound'. Purcell reported that he and many others had gone to Cork city and bought seed potatoes for the spring 'at an extravagant price'.[19] It was a prudent gesture.

The Frost had gone by late February, to great communal relief:

> Hail gentle Thaw ! Celestial maid !
> Sent timely to Hibernia's aid...[20]

But the normal rains of an Irish spring did not follow.

The landscape seemed unimaginably desolate, as fish,
birds and animals perished in the cold.

Temperatures remained extraordinarily low, and piercing
northerly winds prevailed. By April the countryside had a
strangely parched look and an eerie silence. Minor streams
were running quite dry, and once again mills were immobilized.
Much of the wildlife was missing. Birds like the woodcock that
over-wintered had been decimated, and many migratory species
had been terribly affected by weather abnormalities elsewhere,
leaving an anonymous poet to grieve:

> No lark is left to wake the morn,
> Or rouse the youth with early horn;
> The blackbird's melody is o'er

And pretty robin sings no more.
No thrush to serenade the grove
And soothe the passions into love,
Thou sweetest songster of the throng,
Now only live in poet's song.[21]

4

'Without rain what is to become of us?': the drought of spring 1740

The extreme drought brought a series of disastrous town fires: in Carrick-on-Suir (100-150 houses destroyed) and in Thurles (20 houses) in April; in Moate, County Westmeath in June ('upwards of 20 houses'); and in Wexford (53 houses) in the month following. But there were compensations: turf was drawn and stacked by the 20th of April in Castlelyons, County Cork, 'and Tom Conah who is now near a hundred years old does not remember turf to be saved this time of the year'.[22]

But the implications of the drought for most farmers not already hit by the gathering potato crisis were frightening: tillage crops sown the previous autumn – wheat and bere barley – were largely or completely destroyed by the end of April in many districts, and the fodder available for cattle and sheep was almost non-existent. The Frost had seen a huge death toll of animals in the field, particularly of sheep in Connacht and of black cattle in the south. 'The cattle are all dying', it was reported from Lismore in late March.[23] A month later a correspondent from north Wexford asked:

> Without rain what is to become of us ? The corn that is sowed is perishing, the corn we have in our haggards is so prodigious dear the poor cannot purchase it... as for flesh meat they cannot pretend to smell to it [sic], they have lost all their sheep long ago, and now their

last stake, their little cows are daily and hourly dropping
for want of grass...[24]

Meat from such scrawny carcasses was relatively cheap and a
tolerable substitute food for some; Catholics in Dublin were
relieved from normal Lenten obligations and permitted to eat
meat four days in the week 'on account of the great scarcity of
fish, roots etc.' – a recognition of the after-effects of the Frost.[25]
The cold dry weather continued into May and the grass-
starved cattle continued to die. In the first few days of the
month it snowed 'smartly' from Cork to Antrim; in Glenarm it
was reported colder than a normal December, and looking
across the North Channel:

> Scotland would afford us a beautiful landscape if it
> did not at the same time make us shudder to look at it.
> It has been covered these three days past with a lying
> snow...[26]

Some rain fell in the middle of May and, clutching at straws,
the Dublin press made upbeat noises about the prospect of
plentiful markets and falling food prices. In fact quite the
reverse was happening: the catastrophic decline in potato
supplies, which at first had not forced up grain prices, was now
having its effect – despite energetic municipal intervention. By
late spring, record prices were being quoted in the markets,
long after the time of the Frost:

> The poor first felt its dire effects with cold
> When coals were at excessive prices sold;
> Then corn and cattle rose to such a rate,
> The rich were pinch'd to purchase bread or meat.[27]

And by the second week of June wheat prices in Dublin were
precisely double what they had averaged during the Frost itself.
To the ordinary citizen what this meant was that the legal size of
the loaf of bread available for one penny or three pennies had
got smaller and smaller. This was because in Dublin, as in most
larger towns, the Corporation operated an 'assize of bread'; this
involved fixing bread sizes each week at a given weight according

The streets were 'so covered with beggars that there is no passing for them'.

to the price of wheat in the city market and such a system was regarded as the best way of preventing bakers and their suppliers from defrauding the public.

The wholesale rise in the price of wheat, oats and barley reflected not just the current supply position, but the dealers' assessment as to the state of things later in the year. During the long weeks of drought it had become obvious that most kinds of grain would be in very short supply after the next harvest.28 And the news from abroad only reinforced this impression: poor harvests and depleted food reserves across Europe offered little hope that overseas supplies would meet the deficit.

By mid-summer 1740 the country was moving towards an appalling social crisis. What the Frost had done to the potatoes, the drought had now done to the much of the grain harvest. In the countryside, the meal stocks of thousands of families were already exhausted, having been used up prematurely to replace the potatoes that had vanished in the soil. With cattle and sheep dying – or at best a wasting asset – small farmers rarely had the resources to buy meal at market, certainly not in adequate quantities. Some turned to the roads – the age-old response in calamitous times – and a mass vagrancy towards the better-supplied towns began; by mid-June the streets of Cork 'were so covered with beggars that there is no passing for them'.[29] But there were also early reports in the London press – amid weather and disaster stories from across Europe – of the poor in Cork beginning to starve to death.[30]

Such stories were however premature. Richard Purcell's comment from north Cork in mid-May was nearer the mark: 'The common people of this country live on sour milk and greens; which, though it prevents immediate death by hunger, will be the cause of great mortality among them'. (The 'greens' he later explained were 'nettles and charnock, a yellow flowered weed which grows among our grass'.)[31] There were isolated reports of bowel disorders brought on by eating rotten potatoes, and throughout the summer there were accounts from Munster of virulent epidemics of fevers and of smallpox, but these were to be mere harbingers of what was to come.[32]

5

Riots and rumours: the threatened breakdown of order

The countryside was waiting for the harvest and better times; by and large it suffered peacefully. The atmosphere in the towns was more explosive. The soaring cost of food had precisely

the consequences that aldermen had feared since the start of
the Great Frost. In times of scarcity hungry townspeople vented
their frustration on grain dealers, meal-mongers and bakers,
and when they turned to direct action the most likely flash-
points were markets or warehouses where food was held in
bulk.

The first flare-up seems to have been at Drogheda in mid-
April. It was a minor but telling incident. In the wake of an
invasion of meal buyers from Ulster so numerous 'that they
seemed to threaten a famine amongst us', a band of citizens
boarded a vessel at the quay preparing to depart for Scotland,
laden with oatmeal; they disabled it, removing the rudder and
sails. The town's alarmed magistrates undertook that no more
food would be exported from the port.[33] Merchants in those
seaports which in normal times shipped out grain risked
inflaming local opinion when they chose to continue such
trading. Merchants in Cork had refused during the Frost to
take contracts to buy grain for export – yet this was not enough;
there was a riot in the city in early May, directed it seems at
wholesalers of grain.[34]

The biggest explosion of popular anger came in Dublin,
starting on a Saturday at the end of May:

> the bakers having made but little household bread,
> the populace were so greatly enraged that they broke
> open their shops that night and on Sunday; some sold
> their bread and gave them the money, others took it
> away, and in this manner they went through the city...[35]

On the Monday following, the rioters extended their actions
beyond the city, seizing meal from mills in Harold's Cross and
elsewhere near the city, and reselling it at discounted prices.
Several were killed as troops from the Royal Barracks re-imposed
order. The army continued to patrol the streets and markets
for five days and nights. Hoping to lower bread prices, the city
Corporation did its best to smoke out hoarders of grain and to
police food markets, but prices remained stubbornly high
throughout the summer.

Hunger got the better of people. Bread riots broke out in Dublin.

Of the fourteen men and one woman charged with rioting or food theft in Dublin, five were acquitted, three were publicly whipped, three received three-month sentences, and four were transported for seven years. These four had not done anything peculiarly heinous but were seen to be notorious characters.[36] There was a curious footnote to the affair: while en route to the New World the transportees (who were evidently a spirited bunch) escaped from their ship off Waterford and were last heard of 'out on their keeping' in a wood near Kilkenny. But one of their number, Henry White, whose conviction had been for breaking, entering and stealing from Elizabeth Cavenagh's bakery in Dirty Lane off Thomas Street, rashly chose to venture back to the city. He was re-arrested early one September morning after mugging a gardener in his old haunt of Dirty Lane. He was executed two months later.[37]

There were potentially violent skirmishes in other towns in the course of the summer of 1740. In Belfast a demonstration led the town sovereign to put pressure on a grain merchant to disgorge food stocks onto the market. Threats of trouble in Sligo town led to the local sale of barley due to be shipped to Limerick. In Galway 'the town rose' and seized consignments of ship-biscuit that were being loaded at the quays; army intervention was required to restore order.[38]

Exceptionally high food prices were only one side of the equation of urban distress. Demand for goods and services of all kinds was greatly weakened by the twin factors of falling purchasing power on the part of consumers (urban and rural) and the decline of business confidence among those still with credit or ready money. Craftspeople in most sectors of workshop industry were having to cope with unemployment; there was little or no demand for their products or skills.

Quite apart from the crippling effects of the weather there was war; hostilities with Spain had broken out in October 1739 and were contributing to this 'deadness of trade'. Spanish privateers were capturing significant numbers of ships trading with Ireland, including vessels bringing in grain.[39] There was in addition the unsettling likelihood of a wider war involving France, linked to the dispute over the succession to the Austrian throne.

War with the Continental enemies of Protestant Ireland necessarily caused something of a *frisson* through the political establishment; from Co. Cork Richard Purcell had reported to his English employer in March 1740 how 'the common people' despite the prospect of a famine were 'surprisingly elated with the hopes of an invasion from the Spaniards'. And indeed at this very time the Irish government was being warned by London of the ominous massing of Spanish forces in the far north-west of Spain. But the euphoria seems to have passed quickly. By the end of June Purcell reckoned that his poorer Catholic neighbours were now 'so hard put to it to find wherewith to satisfy their hunger, that they think but little of the Spaniards, or giving any disturbance to the Government'. And it was soon evident that the Spanish force was destined for the Caribbean.[40]

As the depleted harvest ripened, the vista facing rural small-holders across much of the country was ominous. Government and parliament can be severely faulted for not seeing the danger signals as clearly as many down the country did, and for not appreciating that the food crisis could only deteriorate in the following seasons, even if normal weather conditions returned. The Duke of Devonshire and his vice-regal entourage returned to England in May after the Irish parliament had gone into recess for eighteen months, and the country was as usual left in the charge of three Irish-domiciled Lords Justices. The most able of these was Hugh Boulter, Church of Ireland archbishop of Armagh, who had been active both publicly and privately in trying to mitigate the effects of the famine of 1728-29. But that had been primarily an Ulster affair, and Boulter's first loyalties had always been to his Ulster province. Now an old man, would he be able to respond energetically to what was self-evidently a national crisis ?[41]

6
The Arctic returns

L ate August and a much delayed harvest commenced. The drought-stunted wheat was of very poor quality, oats somewhat better. But enough grain was brought to market to

The weavers were no longer able to carry on their work.

ease the scarcity. Prices in the towns started to fall, continuing to do so for about five weeks (not indeed fast enough for some, and in September there was another, less bloody, Dublin riot in that barometer of the city's mood, Dirty Lane). Oatmeal prices were halved in Ulster by mid-September, and by late in the month Dublin wheat prices had fallen by nearly a third. Cattle were only beginning to come back into condition, and with hay promising to be like gold-dust by mid-winter, many were sold off prematurely. In the dairying districts, cows had been so weak after the Frost that at least a third of them had failed to take bull; thus by the autumn it was apparent that there was going to be a drastic reduction in the supply of calves, milk and butter over the following seasons.[42]

Even with the return of somewhat lower grain prices the country faced a hungry winter. There was a simmering anger at various levels of society directed against the farmers and dealers who it seemed were manipulating food markets and grain supplies; there was a warning from Armagh that if 'such vermin' were not controlled 'the poor may be in danger of dying in the street with hunger, and... our very linen trade will sink, the weavers not being able to maintain the necessary hands for carrying on their work...'.[43]

Linen, salted beef and pickled butter were Ireland's chief export earners, and all were highly vulnerable to wartime disruption. On the 3rd of October a proclamation issued forth from Dublin Castle placing for the first time a general embargo on the export of Irish provisions to all destinations, thereby reserving stocks for British naval use and denying them to enemies or potential enemies. The procurement of beef and butter, pork and ship-biscuit had become a vital element as Britain and France edged towards another naval war, and with acute pan-European shortages of the foodstuffs that eighteenth-century war machines depended upon, control of what little was available could have a fundamental bearing on the military outcome. The export embargo was a considerable blow to graziers and dairy farmers, and the uncertainty as to Admiralty needs and contracts provided a further complicating factor.[44] Land values and the flow of rents were threatened. The irony is of course that the embargo was not intended to ease the domestic food crisis; the plight of Ireland's rural poor was not uppermost in the minds of those concerned with winning an Atlantic war with Spain.

The weather meanwhile continued to play strange tricks. There had been a violent storm at the beginning of August 1740 on the eve of the harvest, followed by a far more than usually tempestuous September. Blizzards swept along the east coast in late October depositing 'prodigious' amounts of snow on Belfast, and there were repeated heavy falls of snow across most of the country in the following weeks. At least two storms

Pre-industrial towns depended on the constant activity of mill wheels. The ice brought all production to a halt.

came in the course of November, again followed by rains, snow, or frost. And a massive downpour on December 9th culminated in widespread floods; several houses and 'whole trees' were washed into the Liffey and reports came from Navan of 'the greatest flood in the river Boyne that was ever known in the memory of man'.[45]

A day after the floods, temperatures plummeted. A frost reminiscent of the Great Frost set in, only on this occasion it was accompanied by 'the greatest quantity of snow... that has been known for many years'; the snow was reported to be two foot deep at Armagh, the frost five inches into the ground in County Cork. Again rivers across Ireland – and Britain – were frozen over, 'the people sliding and skating everywhere' on the Liffey.[46] But on this occasion the intense cold lasted only ten days and was broken by yet another storm as temperatures rose sharply. The results were spectacular: great segments of ice cascaded down the Liffey causing havoc along the quays, overturning lighters and causing larger vessels to break anchor. (December 1740 was also a time of disastrous floods in many parts of England and France, and in Holland the dykes burst.) Yet despite the winter inundations, overall rainfall in 1740 reflected the earlier months of drought; the level recorded was less than 40% of that for 1738 or 1739.[47]

The bizarre early winter weather had, not surprisingly, pushed food prices back up to famine levels. Dublin wheat prices as recorded on December 20th were at an all-time high. The widening of the war in mid-December encouraged the minority who were lucky enough to have food in their barns or warehouses to hold onto it in the expectation that things could only get worse. But for people dependent on the market for their food supply, renewed panic set in. There were riots in several southern port towns in November. At Dungarvan a crowd threatened to set fire to a ship if it attempted to set sail with a cargo of barley. In Youghal a crowd was summoned by the beat of a drum and confronted a merchant who was despatching a consignment of wheat to Dublin; he was told to sell the wheat at the price he had paid for it or else have his house pulled down. Further west at Kinsale, a vessel from New York on its way to Cork had been forced to seek shelter. Townspeople demanded that the master should sell off at least some of its New World wheat and flour at knock-down prices. He refused the offer and a crowd, reportedly of two hundred, boarded the ship, cut its sails and brought it by some means to the town quay. However covert help from a local customs officer allowed the ship to escape to Cork.[48]

Such dramatic incidents, like those of the previous summer, can be interpreted in two ways: were they the relatively measured expression of underlying popular anger at the greedy behaviour of merchants and dealers, acting contrary to natural justice and the conventional sense of fair play; or were they no more than the desperate opportunistic actions of people already weakened by malnutrition ? We know too little of the circumstances and character of the participants in these 'riots' to be certain (even the unfortunate Dubliner Henry White remains a shadowy figure), but the occasional references to money being offered for hi-jacked food and to attempts by 'the mob' to direct food into local public markets, would indicate that urban direct action, even in this worst of times, was disciplined and operated according to some informal code, not unlike what which has been well documented in the cases of English bread riots.[49] That this may have been so is the more remarkable given the growing signs of full-blown famine and epidemic that were everywhere about them by December 1740.

7
'Not one dies now for seven that used to': the big relief schemes get underway

As Christmas approached, the record food-price levels in Dublin seem to have acted as a catalyst. To help re-assure the capital's citizenry that something was being done, the Lord Mayor, Samuel Cooke, made a well-publicized visit to the Castle on the 15th of December. His declared purpose was to consult with the Lords Justices, Archbishop Boulter, Speaker Boyle and Lord Chancellor Newport, 'on proper measures to reduce the price of corn'.[50] Their response was considerably more robust than hitherto: the Privy Council issued a proclamation on the 22nd instructing the high sheriff in each county to enumerate all stocks of grain being held in farmers' and merchants' hands and to make a return of total cereal stocks in their county. Secondly Boulter, acting in his private capacity, launched a fund to underwrite the cost of an emergency feeding programme for the poor of Dublin. Here, at last, we find the nearest thing to an active government response to the crisis.

The attempt to construct an estimate of national food stocks was hopelessly ambitious; county officialdom lacked the bureaucratic resources to carry out a thorough search of haggards, farm-yards and merchant warehouses in their respective counties, and there was no equivalent to the nationwide constabulary which a century later would gather the first comprehensive foodstock statistics on the eve of the Great Famine. Returns for Counties Wexford and Dublin were made public in January 1741. The totals reported indicate the existence of surprisingly large privately held stocks (though in the case of Wexford it is probable that the returns relate mainly to malting barley).[51] Detailed returns were presumably compiled in a number of other grain-producing counties. Those for most of Co. Louth alone survive: there, over 85,000 barrels of grain – mainly oats – were recorded as being in the hands of some 1,655 farmers, implying that little more than one household in five in the county still possessed significant reserves of food. Yet to contemporary consumers, evidence that there was indeed food, any food, in the countryside seemed confirmation that a limited number of wealthy farmers and dealers were still exploiting the community by holding back supplies from the market in the hopes of securing even higher prices later in the winter.[52] (Some three months later William Aston, MP for County Louth, led a posse which intercepted two boats at Clogherhead that had been attempting to break the embargo and export oatmeal to the Isle of Man; eighteen tons were confiscated.)[53]

The Boulter relief plan was designed to provide free basic rations to those *bona fide* residents of Dublin city who were completely impoverished 'by the deadness of trade and dearness of bread' so that they would have no cause to beg on the streets. This in turn would allow the migrant beggars flooding the capital 'from all parts of the kingdom' to be more easily identified and discouraged.[54] Boulter sought to have a large volume of food made available for an extended period at a single location, and the Dublin city Workhouse in James Street was the obvious choice, being located near the Liberties and on the western edge of the city, even though its main function in normal times was not that of a 'poorhouse' for adults but a 'hospital' for the care of abandoned infants and orphaned children. The

*The hungry began to gather in the shadow of the workhouse,
eager for their free meal.*

institution's governors were directed to sign meal-tickets which
would entitle each ticket-holder to one meal per family member
per day. Boulter's initiative therefore went beyond the
emergency schemes that had been mounted during the Frost –
which had involved either the doling out of meal, fuel, or cash,
or the subsidizing of retail markets.

The Boulter scheme came into operation on New Year's Day
1741. By January 12th, 2,902 Dubliners were being relieved
each week-day at the workhouse, 98% of whom had the

appropriate tickets. Numbers fluctuated over the following months. The number of supplicants soared in late March, coinciding with another surge in food prices, and in April and May over 4,400 citizens were being regularly fed. However such was the pressure on funds that ticket-holders were at that stage being restricted to three meals a week.[55] Boulter was credited in some quarters with funding the scheme single-handed – at the cost of £18 stg. per day – but through the late winter a number of prominent clergy and peers, notably Deans Swift and Delany, and Viscount Mountjoy, were mentioned in the press as fund-raising for Boulter's feeding programme. But it was still seen as Boulter's achievement and in March a group of citizens led by the Lord Mayor commissioned the painting of a portrait of the primate 'for his great charities to the poor', which was to be hung in the workhouse.[56]

Food aid, in several cases organized explicitly along Dublin lines, was made available in many lesser market towns in the late winter of 1740-41. Relief projects involving regular distributions of food are known to have operated in Cork, Waterford, Cashel, Clonmel, Castlelyons, Lismore, Bandon, Clonakilty, Drogheda, Enniskerry, Newry, Tuam and Galway, and also it seems in Wexford and Kinsale (significantly all but three of these towns are in the southern half of the country).[57] The relative size of the relief effort in some of these centres may have been considerably greater than in Dublin. In Waterford city, which was then much less than half the size of Dublin, 1,800 were being fed by March and 'not one dies now for seven that used to die before it was set up'. There the food on offer two days a week was boiled oatmeal 'made savoury with pepper and salt, leeks and spring herbs', and on the four other weekdays it was boiled beef with oatmeal added.[58]

There was probably considerable variety in local arrangements: some schemes ran until May Day, some until at least mid-July; some cheapskate schemes relied too heavily on a very watery meat broth, and were despised.[59] The practice of offering unrestricted access to food for the 'deserving' poor was modified in the less severely affected areas – in Newry and in Drogheda, where 500 were sold cooked food at a discount price; and only the sick and disabled were to receive it free.[60]

Outside the towns the initiative rested to a large extent with landowners (or their agents if they were non-resident). Cash hand-outs to the poor, whether by an estate agent or a parish committee overseen by the Church of Ireland clergy, were not uncommon, but much depended on the willingness and ability of intermediaries on the ground to prick the conscience of the rich. The press gave considerable coverage to the leadership role of the Protestant bishops and clergy, and not it seems without reason. But among men of the cloth there were also those who refused to be involved or to contribute to local charity. The vicar of Castlelyons, Co. Cork was doubly scorned – for being close-fisted when others were subscribing to local relief funds, and for acting in this manner despite having recently sold two hundred barrels of potatoes at a great price.[61] What made matters worse was that such a large horde of potatoes was likely to have been acquired by him from the parish as tithes paid in kind.[62]

Most of the philanthropic activity of that black spring has gone unrecorded, and we know almost nothing of the reactions of the poor to such displays. However something of the popular appreciation of families who acted with conspicuous generosity is caught in contemporary Irish poetry such as that by Sean O Conaire, the parish priest of Cloyne, in his 'Lament for the potatoes in the year of the big frost 1739':

> Worthy are the deeds which the elderly Barrys did,
> The wisemen of the land and the noblemen of the
>   Powers,
> They released the bondage and the harsh fetters
> From the people who were imprisoned because of
>   lack of food.[63]

This reputation for generosity was confirmed some years later when visitors to the Bride valley in east Cork were told by an innkeeper how Col. Redmond Barry 'was the life of the country around him, and in the late hard times... supported numbers that must have otherwise perished.'[64]

O Conaire also praised his estimable neighbour, the Church of Ireland bishop, George Berkeley:

> There is alms and humanity with the Bishop of Cloyne,
> And may God call him to heaven...
> Poets and sages will truthfully say
> That alms were given in Cloyne.[65]

Berkeley's activities in Cloyne were not restricted to conventional aid; he experimented with simple remedies to stem the virulence of famine-induced dysentery in early 1741. He advocated the use of powdered rosin:

> in a little fresh broth, every five or six hours, till the bloody flux is stopt... If after the blood is staunched, there remains a little looseness, this is soon carried off by milk and water boiled with a little chalk in it.[66]

His episcopal neighbour in the small town of Cashel, Theophilus Bolton, in addition to overseeing the feeding up to 1,000 poor each day, gave wine, 'strong cordials' and medicines procured in Dublin to those who were ill. The cost of the feeding programme was split halfways between Bolton and other local subscribers, and the archbishop arranged for a special house to be set aside for the sick and infirm – what in the next century would called a fever hospital.[67] And Edward Synge, the elderly archbishop of Tuam, also achieved a reputation for great compassion; when he died in the summer of 1741, it was said of him that:

> Where thy blest dome auspicious rear'd its head
> No want appear'd, unnumber'd crowds were fed...[68]

Bishop Berkeley was never shy of instructing the landed gentry as to their duties; in May 1741 he observed to a friend how 'it were to be wished [that] people of condition were at their seats in the country during these calamitous times, which might provide relief and employment for the poor'.[69] His call for 'people of condition' to live on their estates had been a

The 45 metre high obelisk at Castletown, Co. Kildare: suggestive of the sheer enormity of the crisis.

theme in his earlier writings and those of his circle, but it had a particular resonance in 1741. Estate agents and rent receivers, clergy and well-regarded chief tenants, could not hope to extract from an absent landowner the funds or the commitment that a landowner in residence, amidst visible suffering and distress, might be prepared to give.

But there was no guarantee of particular generosity in those who were on-the-spot witnesses: Sir Richard Cox, parliamentarian and improving landlord, observed the death and destruction of Catholic small-holders in his corner of west Cork with grudging concern: 'God Almighty protect them who are yet untouched... The Papists though they are bad members in this society, are yet better than none'.[70] It is a difficult point to prove but it is probable that resident landowners (and ex-landowners) with deeper local roots than Sir Richard Cox were on balance more disposed to charitable action than men with short Irish pedigrees. Perhaps it is a coincidence but the most prominent gentry victims of famine fevers in 1741 were members of old families –

Bryan MacMorrough Kavanagh of Borris, County Carlow and his brother Henry, and Robert Blake of Ardfry, County Galway.[71] Among those with shallow roots it was the clergy of the Established Church and estated women who seem to have particularly distinguished themselves.

The most impressive female philanthropic initiative was undoubtedly that undertaken by the widow of Speaker William Conolly, builder of Castletown House, the greatest private residence ever built in Ireland. By March 1740 Katherine Conolly had decided to erect a huge obelisk on the sky-line a mile north-west of the great house, to be mounted on a set of superimposed arches. The intention was of course that the beautification of her demesne would have an immediate social dividend; the demand for labour to build the gigantic monument would give timely relief to distressed families in the neighbourhood. The resulting structure was admired as a noble work in every sense, and remains a strangely elegant physical landmark of the crisis. John Mapas, head of an old south County Dublin family and probably himself a Catholic, funded a similar relief scheme on Killiney Hill, employing 'the poor' in 1741 to build a huge wall enclosing the hill and to erect an obelisk on its summit.[72] There were doubtless other such schemes under way by the summer of 1741:

> for all that can work, the proper charity is to provide labour for them to be paid with ready money, which would keep them and their families from begging and starving, with this view several gentlemen have employed all that offer themselves for labour, having ordered new and more work to be done than otherwise they would have done.

The work being advocated was 'paving, fencing, draining, making roads or canals, cleaning harbours &c which could employ all that would work, and clear the country of strolling vagrants'. It is quite possible that such schemes replaced the free doles that had operated in the spring as it became clear that the crisis was no temporary blip, and since 'giving charity to those that are able to work without requiring work from them is an encouragement to idleness'.[73]

It was a familiar argument, and one that had only temporarily been eclipsed by the enormity of food shortage. It was re-emerging as a conventional wisdom by the summer of 1741. But just as the resort to a public-works solution for famine relief was to be horribly inappropriate in 1846, so obelisk-building and such like in 1741 had its obvious limitations: many of those in need were too sick or simply too weak to work, and therefore employment schemes were, to put it mildly, an inappropriate response to their plight. For by the beginning of 1741, the accumulated months of bad food, under-nourishment, insanitary living and constant begging had led the country to the almost inevitable consequence: the appearance of a cluster of deadly diseases on an epidemic scale.

8
'The poorer sort die like rotten sheep': the medical crisis

There was no shortage of educated physicians available to cater for the medical needs of the well-to-do in mid-eighteenth century Ireland. How much they contributed to the physical well-being of their patients is another matter, for most of the medical theory on which their diagnoses were based was false. However they were able to perform a range of services for their patients which eased the scourge of illness and pain. A few of these doctors were committed empiricists, products of the new scientific culture and keen to observe accurately patterns in the environment in general and in human pathology in particular; from such disciplined observation they felt able to proceed to formulating theories about disease.

*Rutty was unique in his concern to document
the collapse in the country's health.*

The most distinguished medic of this kind to witness Arctic
Ireland and its aftermath was John Rutty, an English-born Quaker
who had come to Dublin in 1724 and was to remain there, a
successful doctor and respected polymath, until his death half a
century later. His *Chronological history of the weather and seasons,
and of the prevailing diseases in Dublin,* based on forty years of
'diaries constantly kept both of the weather and diseases', was
published in 1770. It includes the only detailed contemporary
account of the interplay between weather and disease during
the 1740-41 crisis, most of it based on his own observations.[74]
While his analysis of disease patterns was unsophisticated if

compared with that of William Wilde, the outstanding medical
analyst of the Great Famine a century later, Rutty's work
represents nevertheless an intellectual revolution in this field in
its recognition that accurate observation, especially over many
years, is the first stage in trying to understand social and natural
phenomena.

Rutty distinguished four distinct diseases present in the course
of the crisis – smallpox, 'bloody flux' (dysentery), malignant or
spotted fever (i.e. typhus), and intermittent fever (probably
relapsing fever) – each with a distinctive pattern of symptoms.
Rutty's comments about the ebb and flow of these sicknesses
relate in the first instance to the position in Dublin but they can
be applied to the whole country and all classes. His remarks on
1740-41, a small part of the book, are tantalizing and not without
some ambiguity, but are far more specific and reliable than the
brief testimonies of other witnesses. Indeed Rutty provides
almost the only narrative of the medical history of the crisis.

In the course of 1740 newspapers had made little reference
to the occurrence of life-threatening diseases. But from
December 1740 until the following August we find a welter of
references to the prevalence of fevers, fluxes and/or smallpox
in different parts of the country. However the perspicacious
Rutty dated the commencement of the cycle of disease to at
least six months earlier. In his view the first deadly visitation of
the crisis was that of the child-killing smallpox, the transmission
and virulence of which he linked to the long drought of spring
1740.[75] Then from July 1740, dysenteries spread 'first among
the poor (several of whom died for want)', then to richer folk; it
'raged greatly', especially in the late winter of 1740-41. A third
layer of distress had been added in autumn 1740 when one or
more strains of fever appeared, subsided somewhat in the course
of the winter, and then resumed with added potency in spring
1741.[76]

Modern research on the pattern of epidemics in communities
where normal levels of nutrition have collapsed would confirm
the plausibility of much of Rutty's comment. It would be quite
reasonable to expect the early appearance of an epidemic like

smallpox, the heightened virulence of which would not be directly related to lowered resistance or poor diet, but would have arisen from a surge in vagrancy and the accelerated spread of infections that regularly re-appeared in a less spectacular fashion.[77] The very localized patterns of such epidemics in years when food supplies were normal is a reminder that in early eighteenth-century Ireland many farming communities, particularly their women and children, had very intermittent contact with strangers from outside the parish. Extraordinary times usually meant vastly greater numbers on the roads and in the towns. Heightened contact between strangers – in crowded streets and lanes, markets and fairs, courts and jails, and places where food or doles were on offer – provided ready opportunity for the transmission of pathogens.[78]

Then came the gastro-intestinal infections, chiefly bacillary dysentery, which usually spread during hungry summers, being associated with the consumption of adulterated food and polluted water. In this topsy-turvy crisis dysentery only achieved its full impact in many districts around mid-winter 1740-41. 'Great numbers of poor people daily die of fluxes, which is owing to their wretched food', it was reported from the midlands town of Birr in early December. Richard Purcell provided a longer view on the state of health in north Cork a week before Christmas:

> We have had a very sickly summer and autumn in this kingdom, which has produced a great mortality, especially among the poorer sort of people; the small pox and fever swept away great numbers in these seasons, and now the flux rages in every part of this county, and is very mortal... [79]

A correspondent from Drogheda a fortnight later spoke in similar terms:

> We have a great mortality among the poor people, who die in great numbers from fevers and fluxes. One poor man buried eight of his family in a few days. This mortality is owing to the badness of the diet, which the poor have been obliged to feed on.[80]

*'The bloody flux' (dysentery) killed up to one
in three of those who caught it.*

Dysentery only arrived in Bishop Berkeley's parish a month
later 'though it had made a great progress in other parts of this
county [of Cork]'. By May he was less specific as to the prevailing
epidemics, referring to 'the endless' distresses of the sick and
poor. He clearly regarded Munster as the epicentre of the
pestilence: 'the havoc of mankind in the counties of Cork,
Limerick and some adjacent places, hath been incredible'.[81]

Dysentery – 'the bloody flux' – was thus the primary scourge,
at least in the southern counties, up until the spring of 1741,
just as it was in other poor regions of Europe in those seasons,
notably Brittany and the Scottish Highlands. The poor in
countryside and town, whose intestinal systems had been upset
by months of unbalanced and often foul and unwholesome
foods, were highly vulnerable to such an immediately debilitating
illness, and the survival chances of children who caught dysentery
were even worse than those of adults. The infection would last
from three days to a fortnight, bringing with it extreme nausea,
body pains, fever, colic, bitterly painful intestinal ulceration
and possibly internal gangrene, accompanied of course by
constant foul-smelling, life-draining bloody diarrhoea. In some
families as many as a third of those affected may have died.[82]

What then of the fevers ? The appearance of 'continuous

Typhus became rampant.
Discovering the first spot
seemed like a death sentence.

fever' was noted by Rutty and others in the final months of 1740 and was possibly a flare-up of typhoid fever, an epidemic spread by infected water or food in autumn seasons after dry summers, and it seems to have been paralleled by outbreaks of what in the next great famine would be called relapsing fever.[83] Whatever the cocktail of fevers in 1740, we know that they were less deadly than the 'malignant' variety which was the centre of comment in the following spring. This 'pestilential' infection was spoken of with markedly greater fear than were the 'fevers and fluxes' of the previous autumn. John Usher, chief agent of the great Burlington estates and based at Lismore, wrote in chilling terms to London in mid-February 1741, describing how:

> a bloody flux and a violent fever rages so [much] all over the country that scarce a day passes that we do not bury fifteen or sixteen even in this small place, they are frequently found dead on the highways... For my own part were it not for the business of this place I would fly for my life.[84]

And in Castlelyons, County Cork, the fever, not the bloody flux, was singled out in early March, being 'so malignant' that the victims 'lie dead several days before they are buried'. A month later the word picture from there was even more shocking: 'the poorer sort die like rotten sheep...'. Even at that point the cause of the terrible fever was being traced back to the Great Frost, or rather to the 'eating [of] the frosty potatoes last spring'.[85]

The assumption that the principal (but not exclusive) killer fever of 1741 was typhus is highly plausible. In the previous year descriptions of fever were unspecific, but by spring 1741 there was repeated mention of the fever being 'spotted' or 'purple'; this is consistent with typhus' distinctive symptoms of under-skin haemorrhages and a prominent rash.[86] Typhus was an infection that could spread easily in the harsh and hungry environment of a 'mature' famine, being effortlessly transferred from the infected faeces of human body lice to new victims by their breathing in the faecal dust or by scratching. Infection by inhalation must therefore have crossed class and nutritional boundaries. But where personal hygiene was very poor, and where cold and chronically malnourished people were living in close proximity to one another, contagious transmission of the disease via the infected lice to all family members was more likely.

Typhus affected both mind and body, producing delirium, vertigo and tinnitus, and all the physical symptoms of high fever. Lasting up to a fortnight, it was distinguished from other fevers by the spotted rash and a bloodshot appearance to the eyes. The immediate cause of death was usually heart failure, and fatality rates from typhus seem to have been much higher than from the other prevalent epidemic fevers, particularly for adult victims and most disastrously so in the case of the old. Its virulence in 1741 was possibly enhanced by reduced levels of immunity that resulted from the long-drawn out inadequacy of the diet in poorer households. Rutty believed that there was a link between the deadliness of the fever and the relative scarcity of food – but unlike the undisputed correlation between nutrition and infection in the case of dysentery, this point remains somewhat controversial among medical historians.

What is not in doubt is that typhus, unlike dysentery, could jump class barriers and bring down those who were perfectly well-fed.[87]

9

Spring-summer 1741: the catastrophe reaches its climax

The most apocalyptic accounts of death and destruction primarily date from the terrible spring of 1741 when dysentery and typhus were scything through district after district. The disaster was reaching its profligate zenith. Writing from his west Cork base in late April Sir Richard Cox described how:

> mortality is now no longer heeded; the instances are so frequent. And burying the dead, which used to be one of the most religious acts amongst the Irish, is now become a burthen: so that I am daily forced to make those who remain carry dead bodies to the churchyards, which would otherwise rot in the open air; otherwise I assure you the common practice is to let the tree lie where it falls, and if some good natured body covers it with the next ditch, it is the most to be expected. In short, by all I can learn, the dreadfullest civil war, or most raging plague never destroyed so many as this season. The distempers and famine increase so that it is no vain fear that there will not be hands to save the harvest...[88]

Cox compared the crisis with 'the dreadfullest civil war' and Berkeley in an undated letter spoke similarly: 'in all this province of Munster great devastations are made by bloody fluxes, fevers, and want, which carry off more than a civil war'. And Philip

'the dead have been eaten in the fields by dogs
for want of people to bury them.'

Skelton, the literary curate of Monaghan parish, later reported that 'it is computed by some... that as many people have died... within these two years past, as fell by the sword in the massacre and rebellion of [sixteen] forty one',[89] the *annus terribilis* of Protestant collective memory. He claimed in print that there were:

> whole parishes in some places... almost desolate; the dead have been eaten in the fields by dogs for want of people to bury them. Whole thousands in a barony have perished, some of hunger and others of disorders occasioned by unnatural, unwholesome, and putrid diet.[90]

A pen-sketch of the situation around Cashel in May was also published in a pamphlet, and despite the rhetorical style it probably does not unduly exaggerate:

> Multitudes have perished, and are daily perishing... some of fevers, some of fluxes and some through downright cruel want, in the utmost agonies of despair. I have seen the labourer endeavouring to work at his spade, but fainting for want of food and forced to quit it. I have seen the aged father eating grass like a beast... the helpless orphan exposed on the dunghill,

and none to take him in for fear of infection... the hungry infant sucking at the breast of the already expired parent.[91]

And from Galway in early July came news that:

the fever rages so in this town, that physicians say 'tis more like a plague, and refuse to visit for any fee whatever.

This information, sent in a letter to the *London Daily Post*, went on to report that:

Gentlemen carry little boxes of tar with them, and there is scarce a shop without some of it in their windows, and sprigs of wormwood.[92]

Bishop Berkeley would have approved.

The socially prominent victims of epidemic drew particular attention. Sir Alexander Staples, a leading Dublin merchant, and the wife of John Clancy, the Temple Bar shipper, both died in July (Mrs Clancy having been 'extremely charitable to the

*'I have seen the aged father eating grass like a beast . . .
the hungry infant sucking at the breast of the already expired parent'.*

poor'). Two of the three judges on the arduous Munster spring circuit of 1741 also succumbed: Prime Sergeant Bettesworth in Cork, Chief Baron Wainright after returning to his home in Mount Merrion; and the venerable Lord Chief Justice, Sir John Rogerson, after completing the north-east circuit in August, apparently died of fever in Dublin 'lamented by the poor to whom he was a constant benefactor'.[93] Such casualties ensured that the normally thronged assizes, the highlight of county life, were thinly attended that summer. Indeed the Galway assizes and the accompanying Galway Races were re-scheduled and moved to Tuam on grounds of public health. [94]

The fear of disease being spread at the county assizes was not mere paranoia. The normally claustrophobic conditions of eighteenth-century courts were exacerbated by the vast number of prisoners being paraded before the judges. The Lord Chancellor expressed well-grounded fears for the health of his colleagues 'worn down' by the vast numbers to be tried; in the Munster circuit they were 'grievously offended daily with miserable spectacles, expiring wretches and noisome [sic] smells'. Most of those presented had been committed on remand for the theft of cattle or of food:

> provisions are so scarce that 'tis impossible to supply all, and there is now scarce a night passes without accounts from different parts of the country of cows, sheep or some kind of provisions being stole, and the jails are already so full that the consequence is greatly to be dreaded.[95]

Eighteenth-century jails were notorious breeding grounds for all classes of fever, even when they were not full. And they were very full in 1741: two hundred had been thrown together in the modest Cork county gaol by February awaiting trial, and by the time of the assizes in March there were upwards of four hundred. Wexford jail, with forty-seven felons on remand, was reported not to have held so many 'since the Revolution', and the same was being said of Drogheda jail prior to the spring assizes. There, the prisoners made a determined effort to break out, in the hope, some said, that 'hunger will break stone walls'. At the Kildare summer assizes in August, of the sixty-four indicted for felonies, 'great numbers' were acquitted and 'being extremely poor, were immediately set to liberty, without paying their fees'. The local correspondent welcomed such leniency – not on some principle of natural justice but on the grounds that while confined in jail the prisoners had suffered 'in an uncommon degree the general calamity of hunger and sickness'.[96] Four men convicted at Limerick assizes of cow and horse thefts were treated 'as objects of mercy' because of 'the great scarcity' – and 'burnt in the hand, and turned out of court' for their troubles.[97]

Dublin's Newgate prison had become a particularly gruesome charnel-house of disease by February 1740-41, being packed with over 140 city and county prisoners, mostly on remand. They were bottom in line for scarce resources. Those from the city were receiving a sixpenny loaf of bread every eight days (then weighing only four pounds) – 'a poor substance (God knows) in this dreadful season' – and the county prisoners absolutely nothing from the public purse. Their plight was recognized. *Faulkner's Dublin Journal* (published only a short distance from the jail) used shock tactics on its readers to rouse their compassion:

> four [prisoners]... have within these few days died through real hunger, as it most shockingly appeared from their having eaten their tongues almost out of their heads, and many other such spectacles of poverty, that their eyes are falling out, and their bones piercing their skins.

Faulkner subsequently reported a steady trickle of donations, which were passed on to the prisoners in the form of bread, cheese, and beer, chiding his readers that:

> we should not see such numbers of our fellow creatures in abject poverty, starving in our streets or pining and rotting in our jails, where there are many confined for taking the bare necessities of life, by the first law of nature, self preservation.[98]

*Four lucky men were merely branded in the hand,
and turned out of court for their troubles.*

We can indeed assume that the great majority of those held in prison around the country had been engaged in the theft of food. The law fell heavily on some of these: the press reported a total of sixty-seven capital convictions at the various county assizes in 1741, about treble the average reported for the previous two years, and the number for the assizes in 1742 was more than double that again, suggesting a huge legal overhang from 1741. Such severity of punishment was entirely untypical of the period: 82% of all death sentences in the decade 1739-48 were handed down in 1741 and 1742. Sentences of transportation to north America also peaked in these two years (484 for the country as a whole); that level was about double the norm.[99]

There were further outbreaks of violence during the sickly months of 1741, the most notorious of which were food riots in the Dublin Liberties in March, and in Sligo and Carrick-on-Suir in April. The Carrick incident was much the most serious. A crowd, said to be a thousand strong and probably largely composed of the town's weaving fraternity, tried to sabotage the shipment downstream of a cargo of oats destined for the poor of Waterford city. The local justice of the peace accompanied by eighteen soldiers intercepted the irate citizenry on the Suir bridge, but lost control of the situation. The soldiers opened fire and five of the rioters were shot dead.[100]

Some of the largest and least documented actions involved remote communities in the west, where the storming of beached vessels carrying food or other cargoes was not unknown. Thirty-eight islanders from Inishbofin, Co. Mayo ended up in Castlebar gaol, charged with deliberately beaching and plundering a brig from Antigua 'richly laden with sugar, cotton and ginger...'.[101] Their fate is not recorded.

The great fear among 'the richer sorts' by the summer of 1741 was that the epidemics would reach up the social ladder; this led to a new intolerance of vagrants and beggars. The numbers tramping the roads at that time may have been no greater than in the previous year, but now as purveyors of typhus they presented a more immediate threat to the comfortable classes. They would have to be controlled, corralled and preferably expelled from the towns. At the summer assizes in Maryborough (Portlaoise) 'not one beggar was permitted to stay in the town, by which means there was no infection there.'[102] In mid-August there was a purge of Dublin vagrants: the Lord Mayor issued a proclamation ordering the arrest of all idle vagrants, and the next day 'a great number were taken up and carried in the city carts to the Workhouse'.[103]

Dumping the vagrants in that creaking institution was grossly irresponsible. No longer a centre of emergency food-aid, it was over-full with its normal type of inmate, the abandoned babies and children of city and country. The folly of sending diseased beggars to join them was evident in the exceptional death rate in the Workhouse, bad even by its appalling record: in the year beginning June 1741 more children died in the institution (700) than were actually admitted into it.[104]

Other innocent victims of circumstance were the many insolvent debtors (usually small-scale dealers and artisans) who in that era faced open-ended imprisonment until their debts were settled. Despite the regular championing of their cause by the Charitable Music Society (through the promotion of charity concerts in Dublin), conditions in the debtors' prisons during 1741 were desperate. The largest such jail in the country was the Marshalsea near Christ Church Cathedral in Dublin. No food was provided for the inmates there until the Lord Mayor installed a boiler in June. But despite this it became one of the last scenes of carnage during the crisis: over a hundred debtors were reported to be at risk from a 'raging distemper' in early September.[105]

10
'The earth is loaded' : the return of plenty

Weather in the spring and summer of 1741 continued out of kilter but not to the same sinister extent as in previous seasons. There had been violent storms in late January,[106] followed by another rainless spring; the drought hit the much weakened livestock population and posed a threat to the '41 harvest. March weather was 'serene, dry, frosty and dusty... blasting and burning the grass', and drought conditions lasted with little remission until late June. There was another spate of serious town fires: Cavan in April, Navan and Omagh the following month. The Omagh fire razed almost the whole town to the ground, leaving little more than a church, gaol and court-house standing.[107] Only in late June were there reports of widespread rains, in time to give reasonable potato yields but devastating the hay crop in the south. But rain or no rain, it was remembered as a very hot summer.[108]

In the first week of July grain prices at last began to tumble; old wheat, hoarded surreptitiously in merchants' warehouses, came flooding into the markets.[109] The first of the newly harvested Irish wheat was sent into the Dublin market on the 25th of July by a Lucan farmer, William MacCarthy, with appropriate street theatre:

> The populace, to their inexpressible joy upon the prospect of being delivered from their former wants,

had a piper playing, and a number dancing round the
sack of corn, from six in the morning till market
hours.[110]

This sense of elation moved Laurence Whyte, city poet and
mathematics teacher, to his quill:

> Is this a dream ? Or can we trust our sight
> That corn is fall'n, and bread increased in weight ? [111]

One Strabane veteran reckoned it the most plentiful harvest in
more than sixty years:

> the earth is loaded; potatoes never so many nor ever
> so good... I do assure you of peace and plenty at
> home, I mean the North of Ireland, where we are
> more industrious than any of the other provinces... [112]

Whatever the explanation, Ulster did emerge from the crisis
earlier and less badly scarred than elsewhere. One writer in the
province had noted in the latter part of 1740 that the critical
factor for Ulster had not been the loss of the potato at the time
of the Frost, but rather a history of wretched harvests in the
province, stretching back a dozen years, and of low reserves of
grain being carried by rural households from one year to the
next:

> In some of the bad years [recently], we must have
> been under the sad calamity of a downright famine,
> had it not been for the supply we had from other
> parts. This is evident from the present year [1740];
> for of how great service was the little that was imported
> (in comparison of some former hard years' import)
> tho' we wanted much more.[113]

And even if things got much worse in the following season,
there was one regional characteristic which clearly helped to
soften the effects of the climatic crisis on poorer families in
rural Ulster: the northern diet was centred on oatcake, coarse
bread and stirabout, and as a consequence the regional economy

The harvest was greeted with inexpressible joy. They danced around the corn sacks.

was able to draw on a network of commercial food exchanges in times of local shortage, both inter-provincial and international, unlike many areas in the south where there was a critical seasonal dependence on the potato, local shortages of which were not so easily dealt with. Rural Ulster folk were in a similar position to the town and city-dwellers of the south: when local food shortages threatened – as had happened regularly before 1740 – merchants in the larger ports were usually able to place orders for grain, meal or flour with correspondents as far afield as the Baltic or the middle colonies of America in time to prevent acute distress building up in their hinterlands. But with the Europe-wide grain scarcity of 1740 the normal surplus areas – notably the southern Baltic – could offer nothing, and usually reliable English sources like East Anglia were not much better placed.

George Faulkner, editor of the *Dublin Journal*, had gloomily warned his paper's readers in October 1740 that 'we can have no relief from abroad', the only light on the horizon being that some few ships were 'daily expected from America'. Indeed only the New World offered the prospect of relief at a time when Irish grain production had fallen so desperately below requirements. The import of grain from that quarter was only a very recent development and had heretofore been modest in scale.[114] In the twelve months ending March 25th, 1741 wheat and flour to the official value of about £37,000 was imported direct from the American colonies into Ireland. Irish ship movements to and from Philadelphia and other American ports were anxiously monitored by the newspapers and presumably by the public at large – for example the despatch in December 1740 of twelve vessels chartered by a group of Dublin merchants, led by Clancy of Temple Bar, coinciding with the time when local food prices were at their highest. The repeatedly optimistic predictions of shipping arrivals and their likely impact on local food prices must have strained the credulity of the readers of the Dublin press. Nevertheless when more isolated grain markets were suddenly relieved by sea the impact was considerable; five vessels, presumably from America, reached Galway in early June 1741 'to the great relief of the poor of that country'.[115]

These American supplies constituted about four-fifths of all grain imported into the country in the first year of the crisis. For multitudes in rural Ulster and the southern towns, the American trade was a lifeline, even though the quantities imported were small by the standards of normal years; high as prices were, the possibility of American relief had acted as a brake on food price inflation.

Grain imports to Ireland in the year *after* March 25th, 1741 were nearly five times greater than in 1740-41 in terms of value, and even more so in volume. This reflected not greater Irish need but a dramatic improvement in supplies, particularly from England during the summer of 1741; at that time ships from the likes of Yarmouth and Chichester were bringing over large quantities of cereals to the Irish east-coast ports. By contrast, American imports rose only slightly above the previous year's

levels; they formed less than one-fifth of the total grain imported
into Ireland in 1741-42.[116]

The story of the Great Frost ends as it had begun – with a
meteorological bang. In early September 1741 exceptional
floods in Leinster brought down bridges, damaged mills, swept
away cabins and houses; it was perhaps literally the last straw
for some. Others however saw in the event the purging of the
fever at the end of famine and a return of public health. And
so, for a while at least, it was to be. The quality of the 1741
harvest was very mixed – winter-sown grains cut in July and
August were abundant, but oats and potatoes were in many
districts inadequate, thanks to the early summer drought.

But there was no longer a food crisis. As happened so often
in the wake of a famine, seasons of rare plenty were to follow
over the next two years.[117]

> Our isle's from famine and contagion free,
> What now remains but song and harmony...

The 'song and harmony' of the following winter was indeed not
just the poet's flight of fancy, for:

> ...Devonshire, to make it more complete,
> Has brought us Handel in his science great...

Appropriately, a number of the Dublin concerts associated with
Handel during his celebrated nine-month stay were fund-raisers
for the evergreen cause – imprisoned debtors in the city's
jails.[118]

11

'Ireland will not recover this heavy blow in half a century'

W hat was the balance sheet at the end of twenty-one extraordinary months ? The survivors of it all carried into folk memory a bitter association of frost with suffering; when sudden frosts hit the country in the following generation, there seems to have been momentary and understandable panic. In 1784, at another time of frost and scarcity, the west Kerry under-tenants of Trinity College prayed that the Board would be as charitable as in 1741, 'which bountiful charity enabled our predecessors and the successors of them to have the honour of being your undertenants to this fatal year'. And the memory certainly carried into the nineteenth century: William Harty, writing eighty years later, said that the events of 1740-41 had 'made an impression so indelible that even after the lapse of more than half a century, I have heard the old describe them with feelings of horror'. Eugene O'Curry, writing ninety years after the event, told of how his grandfather had been involved in Clare with 'his horses and sledges in carrying the victims of the plague from all parts of the neighbouring district and burying them'. And even that tortured Machiavelli of the Great Famine, Sir Charles Trevelyan, commented at length in his *Irish Crisis* (1847) on the *bliain an áir*.[119]

How many of Ireland's 2.4 million inhabitants did not survive to tell the tale ? Those trying to make an estimate at the time wrote of 'a third', 'nearly a half ', or even of a half of the 'labouring people' or 'cottiers' being dead, and spoke of an impending or actual labour shortage:[120]

What tho' the soil a plenteous harvest yields,
And lavish hoards o'erspread the fruitful fields,
Ev'n this augments the griev'd Hibernia's pain,
Her sons scarce num'rous to collect the grain.[121]

Can we make any precise estimates of the death toll? No hospital
or poor-house record survives. Probably such documentation
never existed. There is only the stark evidence of the graveyard. Indeed even the documentation relating to the graveyard is very fragmentary, being restricted exclusively to the
burial records of several dozen Church of Ireland parishes, all
of which are east of the Shannon. A poor barometer of the fate
of the poor during the crisis might be one's first assumption,
but in fact the story embedded in these registers is important
and surprising.[122]

In Dublin, the most extensive death registers are those for
St. Catherine's parish (which sprawled across the artisanal south-
west of the capital), and, to the south and east of the city centre,
for St. Kevin's and St. Peter's. In these communities (which
were largely if not predominantly Protestant at that time) the

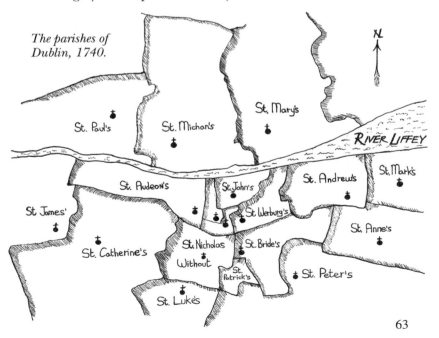

*The parishes of
Dublin, 1740.*

N

St. Paul's   St. Michan's   St. Mary's

RIVER LIFFEY

St. Audeon's   St. John's   St. Andrews   St. Mark's

St James'   St Werburg's

St. Nicholas   St. Bride's   St. Anne's

St. Catherine's   Without   St. Patrick's   St. Peter's

St. Luke's

most deadly months of the whole crisis were, surprisingly, the time of the Great Frost itself.[123] The direct effects of the cold, whether hypothermia or cold-related infections, more than trebled the normal death rate in January and February 1740. The 'bills of mortality', the municipal tally of burials that were published by the city authorities each week tell a similar story – a near trebling of normal monthly deaths.

Rutty explained this heightened death rate as being the result of everyday respiratory infections becoming far more severe during the Frost and proving fatal for 'not only the old, the infirm and asthmatic, but to children also'.[124] The parish evidence bears Rutty out. In St. Catherine's, for example, during February and March 1740, forty-seven children were buried, more than the total for the first eight months of 1741. One wonders to what extent this was a direct consequence of the cold, or whether it could have been due to the fact that people were forced to huddle indoors in congested, smoky rooms.

Later on, famine epidemics did of course reach Dublin – adult mortality in St. Catherine's hit a second, lesser peak in March 1741 – but the overall impression is of death rates in Dublin not unlike those recorded for English and Scottish cities during these wretched seasons. Burials averaged out about fifty per cent higher during the twenty-one-month crisis than for the years 1737-39 in St. Catherine's parish. Rutty, commenting on the prevalence of dysentery in the winter of 1740-41, made the telling observation that the disease 'was less mortal [in Dublin] than in the country which the better care taken of the poor, and of their food, undoubtedly contributed to...'.[125]

This convergence of medical opinion and burial statistics is striking, and Rutty's suggestion that charity, especially in the winter of 1740-41, really did save lives is in the light of these statistics highly plausible. The corollary – that there was higher mortality in the countryside because there was less effective relief there – is more difficult to demonstrate.

Church of Ireland burial registers also survive for a number of Munster parishes; they suggest that in the cities of Waterford

The bodies were 'buried' in a large pit, dug at the back of the church.
There would have been many such mass graves.

and Cork the impact of the crisis was muted enough, with no rise in burial levels in St. Patrick's, Waterford, and a modest rise in Holy Trinity parish in Cork city.[126]   Either these Munster cities were remarkably insulated from what was occurring in their hinterlands or, as seems more probable, these registers do not record the burials of the poorer and more decidedly Catholic elements within their communities. For example, it is striking that as early as April 1740, in what was the earliest reference in any newspaper to famine deaths, an isolated report from Cork claimed that 'many of the poorer sort of people die with hunger'.[127] And many years later it was stated that:

> in the summer after the hard frost, there was a large pit dug at the back of the green in Shandon church-yard [in the city], where several hundred indigent persons were buried for want of money to purchase graves for themselves.[128]

Jany 10th Burid sister Abbolstown.

Jan.^{ry} 22 Burid son of from Dublin

March 18th Burid Fra a poor labourer

March 25th Burid

How does one begin to compute the death toll? By confronting the stark evidence of the parish register and the graveyard.

In the industrial town of Bandon, the burial registers suggest a grimmer picture than for the cities: recorded burials in the town's two grave-yards during the crisis were more than double those of 1737-39.[129]

There are only a couple of surviving parish registers that seem to catch the true dimensions of what was happening in Munster – one for the cathedral parish of St. Mary's in Limerick, the other for Macroom in County Cork. Both of these seem to have been more ecumenical than the norm in that they appear to have included all parish inhabitants that were interred in the Church of Ireland-administered burial ground, not simply those who had been members of the congregation or whose families could afford to pay for graves. And even if not all Catholic deaths in these parishes were recorded – for example those of anonymous beggars from outside the parish – this evidence is still the nearest we can get to a month-by-month measure of the intensity of epidemic and mortality. In both parishes, burial levels during the crisis years were more than four-fold the 1737-39 average, the surge only occurring in the final weeks of 1740. In Macroom, burials reached a peak between December and March, in Limerick city between February and July 1741.

The remarkable contrast in the implied death rate between parishes in Limerick and Waterford cities cannot merely be explained by the inclusion or exclusion of Catholic casualties; there can be little doubt that the larger and more congested walled city on the Shannon suffered far more severely than its south-eastern rival, where an imitation of the Boulter food scheme had quickly got off the ground. One correspondent from Limerick in June 1741 spoke of the recent terrible pestilential fever there: 'it was computed that 700 were sick at one time in this town'.[130] The Waterford region may by contrast have got off relatively lightly.

Parish register evidence is lacking for Connacht, but the impression given by newspaper reports is of a rising, dysentery-driven, death rate in the late winter and spring of 1741, and then a virulent typhus which peaked relatively late in the summer.[131]

What of Ulster in this sea of sickness ? The death rate was certainly above normal in a cluster of parishes close to Lough Neagh for which evidence survives, and in the majority of these burials were highest between February and April 1741, thus conforming to the mortality cycle further south.[132] In the large linen-weaving parish of Blaris, there were 152 fatalities between January 1740 and August 1741, half of which were of children, but in the spring of 1741 the adult proportion rose steeply, suggesting the lethal presence of typhus in the Lagan valley.[133]

Only one attempt at actual measurement of fatalities has come to light. As the crisis ebbed the Church of Ireland minister of the parish of Cullen on the Tipperary-Limerick border in the Golden Vale:

> took a list of all the parishioners, and by the most exact account, found they amounted to 666 persons, and that 252 of that number died of the same distempers... and that 414 were only left alive: by the

*He 'took a list of all the parishioners, and by the most exact
account, found . . . that 414 were only left alive'.*

said list it appears that several whole families have
died, and that [of] others that consisted of four, five
or six persons, only one of a family has been left
alive.[134]

A collapse in the population of the whole island, or even of the
province of Munster, of the order suggested there, 38%, would
indicate a disaster of quite shocking proportions, the effects of
which would indeed have borne out Cox's prediction in April
that 'Ireland will not recover this heavy blow in half a century',
or Berkeley's in May that 'the nation probably will not recover
this loss in a century'.[135]

However the Cullen 'census' almost certainly gives us an
extreme upper-bound estimate. There are several grounds for

not taking it at face value. Firstly, the county hearth-tax returns in the 1730s and 1740s do not point to such a total collapse in taxable houses, even in the case of County Tipperary; a national estimate of between 13-20% excess mortality for 1740-41 has been suggested on the basis of hearth-tax evidence. In other words out a population of around 2.4 millions – close to half the present-day population of Ireland – between 310,000 and 480,000 people may have perished as a result of the crisis.[136]

There is a strong possibility that the estimate of 252 deaths in Cullen parish may include quite a number of families who had in fact fled their homes, in some cases never to return, in others to drift back the following winter. This is not to suggest that any mass emigration took place but rather that there was a desperate rootlessness among the poor during and after the crisis, with most of their wanderings contained within the island. Yet there were a small minority who managed to travel as far afield as did the Famine emigrants of another age. Some of these maritime travellers brought the fever with them, with predictable consequences: one vessel from Belfast, reportedly carrying the colossal load of 180 passengers and servants, reached New York towards the end of 1740 in a terrible condition, 'great numbers [having] died on the voyage, the rest sick and almost starved...'. That however seems to have been a newsworthy item in 1741, which is perhaps some consolation.[137]

A final point against extrapolating from the Cullen, County Tipperary, figure is the probability that that very district was among the worst smitten in 1741; the Golden Vale may have some claim to have been the Skibbereen of this famine. The district was an area of long-established sheep-farming, with an extremely unequal distribution of farm holdings – a world of huge ranches and microscopic cottier potato gardens. And despite the undoubted philanthropic activities of local grandees like John Damer and the Archbishop of Cashel, the record of the Tipperary gentry in responding to the crisis, which touched not so much their tenantry as their under-tenantry, is a silent one.[138]

12
Lessons learnt and lessons unlearnt

I nsofar as one can legitimately talk of positive outcomes in the wake of such human loss, there were one or two tentative dividends. The winter management of potatoes by all classes of farmer appears to have changed, and deeper storage pits were dug thereafter; no mass destruction of potatoes by frost is heard of again.[139] The construction of large public granaries, which was widely discussed during the crisis, was in a few cases acted upon, notably in Cork city. And at least two very large private granaries were erected in the Dublin region, both of which survive: the 'wonderful barn' at Castletown, put up by the redoubtable Katherine Conolly, a seventy-foot high conical structure of brick and rubble stone which was completed in 1743; and the 'Bottle tower' erected in Rathfarnham, County Dublin, apparently in imitation of that at Castletown. Both were presumably for philanthropic purposes as well as providing architectural decoration on their respective demesnes.[140]

Of wider significance was the extension of philanthropic medical institutions in the following years. The Charitable Infirmary in Dublin (the future Jervis St. hospital) was completely rebuilt on Inns Quay in 1740-41; Mercer's Hospital on the south side was extended at the same time. And it has been suggested that the inspiration for establishing a charitable maternity hospital (the future Rotunda) came to the young Bartholomew Mosse as he observed the suffering of child-bearing pauper women in these years.[141] What became Cork's North Infirmary was established in 1744 (adjacent to the emergency burial pits in Shandon church-yard). And Cork's first poorhouse-cum-foundling hospital was opened in 1747.[142]

But in the final analysis what is more remarkable is the

The 'wonderful barn', wonderfully shaped and wonderfully intended, was put up two years later so that no-one here would ever starve again.

absence of major public initiatives. The Duke of Devonshire on opening parliament in October 1741 referred to the famine and sickness and suggested that members might consider ways to prevent any repetition, but the war and Ireland's contribution to its financing were top of the political agenda; indeed hostilities with France and the very real danger of a Jacobite invasion from that quarter left civil concerns a low priority for government and parliament until the last years of the decade. Boulter's death in 1742 robbed the political establishment of the one figure who might have pushed the Irish parliament towards an English-style poor law. The only legislation prompted by the crisis were two acts of no long term importance – one that sought to prohibit the burning of land prior to ploughing, in the hopes that this would increase the supply of winter fodder for cattle, the other a criminal statute to tighten up the penalties against the maiming or killing of cattle.[143]   It was another English-born Church of Ireland cleric, Richard Woodward, who twenty-five years later was responsible for opening the debate on the possibility of a national poor law; this led shortly after to important legislation permitting the establishment of county workhouses.[144]

John Post in his recent Europe-wide analysis of the 1740-41 crisis has argued that Ireland, with Norway, had the highest death rate of any European territory for which data have survived. This was not because Ireland had the greatest temperature extremes but, he has suggested, because of the inadequacy of its welfare and relief infrastructure.[145]   This seems highly plausible, but one might add that perhaps no rural society west of the Elbe had to contend with the extremes of economic inequality that had developed on the grassy plains of lowland Ireland.

How does 1740-41 measure up against the later, more famous, Great Irish Famine ?[146] In terms of *relative* casualties, the older crisis was undoubtedly the more severe, even taking the lower-bound estimate of 310,000 fatalities in 1740/41. Against that, we must not forget that the pre-famine population in 1845 was more than three times larger than the pre-crisis population of 1739, and therefore the volume of suffering and loss in the Great Famine was necessarily much greater, with an excess death rate of at least one million. But the 1840s catastrophe spanned six years; that considered here was concentrated into little more than a year and a half.

Another contrast is geographical: many of the acutely distressed districts in 1740-41 were the most naturally fertile areas of the country; while such areas were also badly affected in the Great Famine, the real blackspots of the 1840s were districts of lower soil fertility and congested population. All the evidence for 1740-41 points to the province of Munster containing the greatest human suffering, but it was the Munster heartland not the western peninsulas that was the crisis epicentre.

As we have seen there was no sudden change in migration patterns as a result of 1740-41. The modest outflow to the American colonies that had begun in the 1710s continued, mainly from Ulster, but mass transatlantic migration only became a popular response to domestic social crisis in the second quarter of the nineteenth century with the coming of cheaper fares. Emigration became an option, indeed the option, for all but the poorest stratum of victims of the 1840s crisis.

The almost complete absence of official documentation on the earlier crisis, compared with the vast public archives and officially sanctioned printed record of the Famine a century later, points to another more fundamental contrast. No Irish administration, whether in the 1740s or the 1840s, had any appetite for large-scale intervention in the welfare of the Crown's subjects, both preferring to operate within minimalist definitions of the function and moral parameters of the state.

But whatever about their respective mindsets, the Irish government of the 1740s was far less able to intervene than their successors in the age of Peel and Russell. The eighteenth-century public service was far smaller, and apart from the Revenue service and the army, the authority of the state was entirely mediated through the gentry, the Church of Ireland clergy, and municipal corporations. Irish government by the 1840s was bigger, more centralized, and had far more efficient eyes and ears throughout the country. With a national police, an army commissariat and a Board of Works, Dublin Castle had an entirely different range of options if confronted by emergency. Most important of all, the country in 1845 was endowed with a recently established and long overdue national poor-law system. In other words, the machinery for large-scale intervention was absent in 1740, present in 1846.

After the 1740-41 famine, the fear of public disorder and of a breakdown in public health led to the gradual extension of the state into preventive and emergency procedures in those harvest failures that threatened a re-run of the Great Frost's outcome. These initiatives had a strongly urban bias, and were designed to moderate the wild swings in urban cereal prices, implying quite wrongly of course that all subsistence problems were tied to the outcome of the grain harvests. However none of the bad years in the second half of the eighteenth century became full-scale crises, and it was not until the end of the Napoleonic wars and the crisis of 1816-17 that the limitations and deficiencies of relief arrangements were recognized and partially addressed by the innovative Chief Secretary, Robert Peel.

A final point of contrast between the two great famines brings us back to the question of memory and public history: the victims of 1740-41 belonged to a turbulent world where catastrophic turns of fate were only too well known; everyone in their fifties and older would have recalled the horrors of the Jacobite wars; those who could read the Dublin or Belfast papers were being given depressing reports of distress across Europe. Nobody saw in the huge Irish carnage a scandal when the weather was so obviously to blame; the generosity of some landlords might be questioned, but nobody faulted government *per se* for what had happened.

The second great famine hit a much altered Ireland: for all the demonstrable problems of the poor, it was possessed of far greater administrative and economic resources than had been the case a century previously, and the literate public of the 1840s were a great deal more numerous and better informed as to social conditions at home and abroad. They were also of course riven by divisions political, religious, and generational over the country's future, and famine policy became an issue of poisoned controversy. Yet nearly all Irishmen by 1847 agreed that it was an outrage that their country should be brought to its knees by famine in an era of peace and relative plenty – unlike the case in 1740 when rich and poor had felt impotent against nature and Providence: for at the time of the Great Frost it was churchmen not politicians who provided an intelligible explanation for disaster to a society that feared God and did not expect very much from distant governments.

Notes

1   John Post, *Food shortage, climatic variability, and epidemic disease in preindustrial Europe: The mortality peak in the early 1740s* (Ithaca, 1985), pp. 23, 52, 60, 63.

2   Robert McKay, ed. *An anthology of the potato* (Dublin, 1961), pp. 44–45 (trans. by Nessa Doran).

3   *Dublin Evening Post* [hereafter *D.E.P.*], 29 Dec.1739-1 Jan. 1739-40.

4   *Belfast News Letter* [hereafter *B.N.L.*], 5 Feb. 1739-40; *Pue's Occurrences* [hereafter *P.Occ.*], 1-5 Jan. 1739-40; *Faulkner's Dublin Journal* [hereafter *F.D.J.*], 19-22 Jan. 1739-40. For news of a 32-foot high icicle in Staffordshire: *F.D.J.*, 26 Feb.-1 March 1739-40.

5   *D.E.P.*, 22-26 Jan.1739-40.

6   *D.E.P.*, 29 Jan.-2 Feb. 1739-40; *P.Occ.*, 26–29 Jan. 1739-40; [London] *Daily Post*, 31 Jan, 1739-40; *B.N.L.*, 29 Feb. 1739-40. Tents were erected on Lough Neagh for what may have been a more inclusive social gathering: *F.D.J.*, 22-26 Jan. 1739-40.

7   *D.E.P.*, 19-22 Jan. 1739-40; *P.Occ.*, 5-9 Feb. 1739-40. For Dublin accidents: *Dublin Newsletter* [hereafter *D.N.L.*], 1-5 Jan. 1739-40.

8   *F.D.J.*, 5-9 Feb. 1739-40; *D.E.P.*, 26-29 Jan. 1739-40.

9   *P.Occ.*, 8-12 Jan. 1739-40; *F.D.J.*, 12-15 Jan. 1739-40.

10   *D.N.L.*, 15-19 Jan. 1739-40; *D.N.L.*, 22-26 Jan. 1739-40; *D.E.P.*, 22-26 Jan. 1739-40; *P.Occ.*, 22-26 Jan. 1739-40. A copy of the proclamation of 19th January is in T.C.D. [Papyrus Case 61/26]. 150 tons of coal had been distributed in Dublin by early February: *D.E.P.*, 29 Jan.-2 Feb. 1739-40.

11   *B.N.L.*, 5 Feb. 1739-40.

12   *An express from Corke, with an account of a bloody battle fought between the mobb of that city and the standing army...* (Dublin, 1729). Cork merchants in 1740 were adamant that they would not risk shipping out corn from the port: John Scott, Cork to Thomas Dillon & Co., 25 Jan. 1739-40 (Dillon papers, N.L.I. Mic. p2762).

13   *D.N.L.*, 5-8 Apr. 1740; *F.D.J.*, 19-23 Feb. 1739-40; *D.E.P.*, 12-16 Aug. 1740. For other examples of absentee gestures during the Great Frost, see earl of Egmont to Richard Purcell, 2 Feb. 1739-40 (Egmont papers, British Library [B.L.] Add. MS 47,005, p. 15 [N.L.I. Mic. p4679]) [Egmont estate]; Sir William Abdy to John Usher, 14 March 1739-40 (Lismore papers, N.L.I. MS 13252/1) [Burlington estate, Co. Waterford]; *D.N.L.*, 26-29 Jan. 1739-40 [Palmerston estate]; *D.N.L.* 8-11 March 1739-40 [Ranelagh estate in Roscommon]; *D.E.P.*, 29 Jan.-2 Feb. 1739-40 [Conolly estate at Ballyshannon].

14   Swift to Mrs Whiteway, 3 Feb. 1739-40 (Harold Williams, ed. *The correspondence of Jonathan Swift*, V: *1737-1745* (Oxford, 1965), p. 179); Post, *Food shortage*, pp. 64-5, 67.

15   Michael Rivers to Thomas Dillon and Co., 1 Jan. 1739-40 (Dillon papers). The cabins which Rivers referred to were presumably sheds built for the purpose of storing potatoes intended for sale; the Dungarvan area was unusual in being already involved in a potato trade to Dublin.

16   Purcell to the earl of Egmont, Kanturk, 22 Jan. 1739-40 (B.L. Add MS 47,001A, f.35).

17   The earliest newspaper reports (*P.Occ.* and *D.N.L.* 8-11 Jan. 1739-40) both spoke of potatoes across the country being 'mostly spoiled in the ground'.

18   Lord Chancellor Robert Jocelyn to the earl of Hardwicke, 29 March 1741, quoted in F.E.Ball, *The judges in Ireland* (London, 1926), II, p. 131; John Keane, Cappoquin to Sir William Heathcote, 21 Apr. 1740 (Heathcote papers, P.R.O.N.I. T.3091/A3/64); Dickson, 'The potato and Irish diet before the Great Famine', in Cormac O Gráda, *Famine 150* (Dublin, 1997), pp. 1-27.

19   Purcell, Kanturk, to Egmont, 22 Feb. 1739-40 (Egmont papers, B.L. Add. MS 47,005, p. 22 [N.L.I. Mic. p4679]). For similar reports from the Castlelyons area of emergency seed being purchased in Dungarvan: William Pearde, Castlelyons, to Francis Price, 20 Apr. 1740 (Puleston papers, National Library of Wales MS 3579D [N.L.I. Mic. p3263]).

20   *F.D.J.*, 30 Dec. 1740-3 Jan. 1740-1. The couplet forms part of a poem on the thaw that was published ten months after the event.

21   Ibid.

22   Pearde to Price, 20 Apr. 1740 (Puleston papers); *D.N.L.*, 15-19 Apr.
      1740; *P.Occ.*, 15-19 Apr. 1740; *F.D.J.*, 15-19 Apr. 1740; *D.N.L.*, 28
      June, 5-8 July 1740; *D.E.P.*, 5-8 July 1740.

23   *D.E.P.*, 23-26 Feb. 1739-40, 12-15 Apr. 1740; *F.D.J.*, 22-26 Apr. 1740;
      Purcell, Kanturk, to Egmont, 2 May 1740 (Egmont papers, B.L.
      Add. MS 47,007A, f.126); John Usher, Lismore, to Sir William Abdy,
      30 March 1740 (Lismore papers, N.L.I. MS 7,179). A Mallow writer
      in October 1740 estimated that a third of the cattle stock and a
      third of the sheep had perished earlier in the year: [London] *Daily
      Post*, 5 Nov. 1740; John Usher, Lismore, to Sir William Abdy, 30
      March 1740; (Lismore papers, N.L.I. MS 7,179).

24   *P.Occ.*, 26-29 Apr. 1740.

25   *F.D.J.*, 26 Feb.-1 March 1739-40.

26   *D.N.L.*, 6-10 May 1740.

27   'Famine' by Laurence Whyte, in *F.D.J.*. 1-4 Aug. 1741. This was
      reprinted in Whyte, *Occasional poems on various subjects... Part the
      second* (Dublin, 1742), pp. 6-9. See Patrick Fagan, *The second city: A
      portrait of Dublin 1700-60* (Dublin, 1986), pp. 177-81.

28   This jump in Irish prices was directly paralleled in England and the
      Low Countries, for the drought was a disaster common to north-
      west Europe, and international grain markets were by this period
      comparatively well integrated: Post, *Food shortage*, pp. 118-9.

29   [London] *Daily Post*, 2 Aug. 1740; David Dickson, Cormac O Gráda,
      & Stuart Daultrey, 'Hearth tax, household size and Irish population
      change 1672-1821', *Proc. Royal Irish Academy*, lxxxii, C (1982), 167.

30   [London] *Daily Post*, 11 Apr. 1740;   also *London Evening Post* as
      quoted in *F.D.J.*, 15-19 Apr. 1740. Cf. John Usher, Lismore, to Sir
      William Abdy, 30 March, 17 Apr., 21 May 1740 (Lismore papers,
      N.L.I. MS 7,179).

31   Purcell, Kanturk to Egmont, 13 May 1740 (Egmont papers, B.L.
      Add. MS 47,001A, f.59); Purcell to Egmont, 13 June 1740 (B.L. Add.
      MS 47,005, p.55 [N.L.I. Mic. p4679]).

32   Post, *Food scarcity*, p. 246; *F.D.J.*, 9-12 Feb. 1739-40; Elizabeth Pearde
      to Francis Price, 15 Aug. 1740 (Puleston papers); Purcell to the earl
      of Orrery, 26 Sept. 1740 (Harvard MS Eng. 218.4F, vol. 7 [N.L.I.
      Mic. p789]). It is possible that the fever referred to was typhus,
      which apparently was very prevalent in south-west England in the
      summer of 1740: Post, *Food scarcity*, p.234.

33 *F.D.J.*, 19-22 Apr. 1740.

34 Scott to Thomas Dillon & Co., 25 Jan. 1739-40 (Dillon papers); Richard Caulfield, *The council book of the Corporation of Cork* (Guildford, 1876), p. 600.

35 *D.N.L.*, 31 May-3 June 1740.

36 *D.E.P.*, 31 May-3 June, 3-7, 14-17 June, 1-5 July, 9-13 Sept. 1740; *D.N.L.* 31 May-3 June, 17-21 June, 1-5, 5-8 July 1740; *F.D.J.* 31 May-3 June 1740; *P.Occ.*, 31 May-3 June, 3-7, 21-4 June 1740.

37 *D.N.L.*, 15-19 July 1740; 5-9 Aug. 1740; 2-6 Sept. 1740; *P.Occ.*, 2-6 Sept., 6-11 Nov. 1740.

38 *D.E.P.*, 21-24 June 1740; *P.Occ.*, 21-24 June 1740; *D.N.L.*, 23-26 Aug. 1740.

39 [London] *Daily Post*, 22 March 1739-40; *D.E.P.*, 27-31 May 1740; *D.N.L.*, 16-20 Sept. 1740. The Mallow writer to the *Daily Post* maintained with some exaggeration that the Spanish had taken 'at least half of all we have exported this year': [London] *Daily Post*, 5 Nov. 1740.

40 Purcell, Kanturk, to Egmont, 21 March 1739-40; 27 June 1740 (Egmont papers, B.L. Add. MS 47,001A, ff.45, 65); Robert E. Burns, *Irish parliamentary politics in the eighteenth century*, II: *1730-1760* (Washington, 1990), pp.50, 52. On the gentry's fear of invasion, see S.J.Connolly, *Religion, law and power: The making of Protestant Ireland 1660-1760* (Oxford, 1992), pp. 249-63.

41 Dickson, 'In search of the old Irish poor law', in Rosalind Mitchison & Peter Roebuck, eds. *Economy and society in Scotland and Ireland 1500-1939* (Edinburgh, 1988), p. 153; Burns, *Irish parliamentary politics*, pp. 61-2.

42 In Aug. 1740 Purcell reckoned that half the cows had failed to conceive, but he gave the slightly less pessimistic assessment of a third in December: Purcell to Egmont, 19 Aug., 30 Dec. 1740 (Egmont papers, B.L. Add. MS 47,001A, ff.72, 102).

43 *P.Occ.*, 11-14 Oct. 1740.

44 The embargo on butter was temporarily lifted at the end of December. For its effects on farm prices, see Purcell to Egmont, 17 Oct., 10 Nov., and 30 Dec. 1740 (Egmont papers, B.L. Add. MS 47,001A, ff.87, 91,101-2).

45 Purcell, Kanturk, to Orrery, 26 Sept. 1740; *D.E.P.*, 5-8 Aug., 28 Oct.-1 Nov., 22-5 Nov. 1740; *D.N.L.* , 20-23 Sept., 21-25 Oct., 27-30 Dec. 1740; [London] *Daily Post*, 4, 23 Dec. 1740; John Rutty, *An essay*

towards a natural history of the county of Dublin (Dublin, 1772), II, p. 471.

46   Purcell, Kanturk, to Egmont, 19 Dec. 1740 (Egmont papers, Add. MS 47,005, p.109 [N.L.I. Mic. p4679]); William Pearde, Castlelyons, to Francis Price (Puleston papers); *P.Occ.*, 16-20 Dec. 1740; *D.E.P.*, 13-16 Dec. 1740; [London] *Daily Post* , 23 Dec. 1740.

47   *P.Occ.*, 20-23 Dec. 1740; [London] *Daily Post*, 25 Dec. 1740; *London Daily Post & General Advertiser*, 3 Jan. 1740-1; Post, *Food shortage*, pp. 63,72. The rain measurements were made in Cork city.

48   *D.N.L.*, 2-6 Dec. 1740; [London] *Daily Post*, 2, 16, 23 Dec. 1740.

49   E.P. Thompson, 'The moral economy of the English crowd in the eighteenth century', *Past & Present*, 50 (1971), 76-136; Neal Garnham, *The courts, crime and the criminal law in Ireland 1692-1760* (Dublin, 1996), pp. 200-1.

50   *P.Occ.*, 12-16 Dec. 1740. For a poetic tribute to Cooke's mayoralty ('... by his wand/Allay'd the Famine spreading o'er the land'), see White, 'Famine', in *F.D.J.*, 1-4 Aug. 1741.

51   40,000 barrels of wheat were returned for County Dublin, and 130,000 barrels of 'corn' for County Wexford: *F.D.J.*, 3-6 Jan., 17-21 Feb. 1740-1.

52   *F.D.J.*, 25-9 Nov., 2-6 Dec. 1740, 3-6 Jan., 17-20 Jan., 17-21 Feb. 1740-1; Rev. Dermot MacIvor, 'An eighteenth-century corn census for Co. Louth', *County Louth Archaeological Jnl.*, XI (1946-8), 254-86. The proportion of grain-holding households in Louth has been calculated as follows: the number of houses paying hearth-tax in the county in 1732 was 7,561, implying a gross house total in the range 8,620 to 10,132 (Dickson, O Gráda, & Daultrey, 'Hearth tax', 149, 177). The 1741 grain returns for the barony of Lower Dundalk are missing, and the county returns did not include the borough of Drogheda; in the 1821 census, these two areas made up approximately 30 per cent of the inhabited houses of Co. Louth (including Drogheda town); on that basis a full return of grain holders for 1741 would have been of the order of 2,150 (although in reality few Drogheda households would have been storing grain).   In the barony of Ferrard, the district lying north of Drogheda, the proportion of stocks held by millers was specifically noted: it amounted to a mere 3% of the oats held locally and 17% of the oatmeal.   For the expansion of tillage in County Louth before 1740, see [Philip Skelton], *The necessity of tillage and granaries . . .* (Dublin, 1741), pp.6-7.

53   *F.D.J.*, 21-25 Apr. 1741.

54   *D.E.P.*, 30 Dec. 1740-3 Jan. 1740-1.

55   *F.D.J.*, 10-13 Jan. 1740-1; *D.N.L.*, 11-14, 18-21 Apr., 9-12 May 1741.
      Around 41 to 42% of those assisted in April and May were designated
      'old', the remainder 'young'. In addition, 'upwards of 100' poor
      were being fed at Trinity College in January: *F.D.J.*, 31 Dec. 1740-3
      Jan. 1740-1.

56   *London Daily Post & General Advertiser*, 1 May 1741; *D.N.L.*, 3-7 Feb.
      1740-1; *P.Occ.*, 13-17 Jan. 1740-1; *F.D.J.*, 21-4 March 1740-1. The
      portrait is now in the T.C.D. picture collection.

57   Cork: *P.Occ.*, 24-28 March 1741; *F.D.J.*, 28-31 March 1741; *D.E.P.*, 9-
      12 May 1741, Caulfield, *Cork*, pp. 607-9; Waterford: *F.D.J.*, 14-17
      March 1740-1; *D.E.P.*, 14-17 March 1740-1, 9-12 May 1741; Cashel:
      D.E.P., 25-28 Apr., 9-12 May 1741; Clonmel: *D.E.P.*, 5-9, 9-12 May
      1741; *F.D.J.*, 5-9 May 1741; *P.Occ.*, 5-9 May 1741; Castlelyons: Pearde
      to Price, 3 Apr., 1 May 1741 (Puleston papers); Lismore: Dean Isaac
      Gervais, Lismore, to Sir William Heathcote, 9 March 1740-1
      (Heathcote papers, P.R.O.N.I. T3091/A3/76); Bandon and
      Clonakilty: William Conner to Henry Boyle, 5 May 1741 (Shannon
      papers, P.R.O.N.I. D.2707/A/1/4/3); Drogheda: *D.N.L.* 12-16 May
      1741; Enniskerry: *F.D.J.*, 5-9 May 1741; Newry: *D.E.P.*, 5-9 May 1741;
      Tuam: *D.N.L.*, 7-11 Apr. 1741; Galway: *D.N.L.*, 31 Jan.-3 Feb. 1740-1;
      F.D.J., 31 Jan.-3 Feb. 1740-1; Wexford: *P.Occ.*, 13-17 Jan. 1741; Kinsale:
      Rev. P MacSwiney, 'Eighteenth-century Kinsale', in *J.C.H.A.S.*, XLIV
      (1938), 111n.

58   *D.E.P.*, 14-17 March 1740-1.

59   *F.D.J.*, 21-24 Feb. 1740-1.

60   *F.D.J.*, 9-12 May 1741; *D.N.L.*, 12-16 May 1741.

61   Pearde to Price, 3 Apr. 1741 (Puleston papers).

62   For a contemporary attack written in Irish on a neighbouring
      minister for levying tithe on the parish priest in 1740, see Liam O
      Buachalla, 'Notes on the history of Conna and Ballynoe', [typescript
      in Cork County Library].

63   McKay, *Anthology of the potato*, p.44.

64   [W.R.Chetwood], *A tour through Ireland by two English gentlemen* (2nd
      ed., Dublin, 1748), p.128.

65   McKay, *Anthology*, p.44.

66   *F.D.J.*, 17 Feb. 1741; A.A.Luce & T.E.Jessop, eds. *The works of George
      Berkeley*, VIII: *Letters* (London, 1956), pp. 248-52. This marks the
      apparent beginning of Berkeley's fascination, medical and

philosophical, with 'tar-water': see N.A.Doherty, 'Bishop Berkeley's tar-water; A physical and spiritual panacea' (unpublished B.A. dissertation, Dept. of Modern History, T.C.D., 1996), p.13.

67   *F.D.J.*, 25-28 Apr., 19-23 May 1741; *D.E.P.*, 25-28 Apr. 1741. Lady Southwell, the *seigneure* of Rathkeale, Co. Limerick, was also dispensing medicines as part of a series of relief measures. And Joseph Fade, the wealthy Dublin Quaker banker, publicized his cure for the bloody flux over many weeks in *Faulkner's Dublin Journal*, it was a mixture of cochineal, cinamon and sugar. Unlike Berkeley, he advised against the consumption of broth.

68   *F.D.J.*, 1-4 Aug. 1741.

69   Berkeley, Cloyne, to Thomas Prior, 19 May 1741 (*Berkeley letters*, p. 252).

70   Sir Richard Cox, Dunmanway, to [? Walter Harris], 23 Apr. 1741 (Armagh Public Library, Lodge MSS).

71   *F.D.J.*, 25-28 Apr., 12-16 May 1741.

72   Desmond Guinness and the Knight of Glin, 'The Conolly folly', *Quarterly Bulletin of the Irish Georgian Soc.*, vi (Oct.-Dec. 1963), 63; James Howley, *The follies and garden buildings of Ireland* (New Haven & London, 1993), pp. 11-14, 196-7.

73   *P.Occ.*, 13-16 June 1741. For a similar plea to the gentry to employ the poor on useful schemes, see *F.D.J.*, 10-14 Feb. 1740-1.

74   John Rutty, *Chronological history of the weather and seasons, and of the prevailing diseases in Dublin* (Dublin, 1770), pp. v-vi, 77-91.

75   Ibid., pp. 80, 337-8; Post, *Food shortage*, p. 244.

76   Rutty, *Chronological history*, pp. 81-2, 85. Rutty assumed that the fever of autumn 1740 was the same as that of summer 1741, but on balance this seems unlikely. Also presumably a problem but not attracting specific contemporary comment was scurvy, the presence of which would have arisen from the sharp decline in the consumption of vitamin-C rich potatoes; it would have been evidenced by large purple skin blotches caused by under-skin haemorrhages, sometimes leading to blackened legs, and by swollen gums (Sir William P. MacArthur, 'Medical history of the famine', in R.D. Edwards & T.D. Williams, eds. *The great famine: Studies in Irish history 1845-52* (Dublin, 1956), pp. 287-8). However there are references to the purple fever in 1741, for example in Limerick (*D.N.L.*, 14-18 July 1741), which suggest scurvy and typhus present together.

77   Laurence Geary, 'Famine, fever, and the bloody flux', in Cathal Póitéir, ed. *The great Irish famine* (Cork, 1995), pp. 79-80; MacArthur, 'Medical history', pp. 271-2.

78   P.A.Worthington, 'Death, disease and famine in pre-industrial Ulster: A study of mortality crisis in two parishes in the Lagan Valley 1725-45 on the basis of Church of Ireland registers' (unpublished B.A. dissertation, Dept. of Economic and Social History, Queen's University, Belfast, 1976), p.23; Post, *Food shortage*, p.246. For graphic comment on large-scale vagrancy and its medical impact in the food crisis of 1816-8, see Geary, 'Famine, fever and the bloody flux', pp. 79-80.

79   Purcell, Kanturk, to Egmont, 19 Dec. 1740 (Egmont papers, B.L. Add MS 47,005, p.109 [N.L.I. Mic. p4679]); *F.D.J.*, 13-16 Dec. 1740. Cf. the correspondent from Cork city who at the beginning of December wrote in the *F.D.J.* of the 'uncommon mortality amongst the poor people, by fevers and fluxes, on account of their poor living, the price of corn being risen to an excessive rate...', quoted in Michael Drake, 'The Irish demographic crisis of 1740-41', in T.W.Moody, ed. *Historical Studies VI* (London, 1968), p.116.

80   Letter dated 3 Jan. in *F.D.J.*, 3-6 Jan. 1740-1, and in [London] *Daily Post*, 24 Jan. 1740-1.

81   Berkeley to Prior, 8, 15, 24 Feb., 19 May 1741; Berkeley to [James], [1741] (*Berkeley letters*, pp. 248-2, 255).

82   Post, *Food shortage*, pp. 260-5; Geary, 'Famine, fever and the bloody flux', pp. 77-83. Note that some of those described as suffering from the bloody flux may in fact have been experiencing the direct physiological effects of prolonged malnutrition, i.e. famine diarrhoea, not dysentery: Post, op.cit., pp. 217-9. Note the similarity with the pattern in the Great Famine, where 'in most parts hard hit..., dysentery was rampant before fever had begun to spread' (MacArthur, 'Medical history', p.286).

83   Rutty, *Chronological history*, pp. 81-3; Post, *Food shortage*, pp. 230, 243.

84   John Usher, Lismore, to Sir William Abdy, 14 Feb. 1740-1 (N.L.I. Lismore papers, MS 7,180).

85   Pearde to Price, 8 March 1740-1, 3 Apr. 1741 (Puleston papers).

86   Typhoid with its tell-tale symptoms of heavy nose-bleeding was it seems active in 1741, at least in Munster (Rutty, *Chronological history*, p. 88; Post, *Food shortage*, p. 232), and Rutty makes it clear that relapsing fever was observed in Dublin in mid-summer of that year (Rutty, op. cit., p. 90).

87   Rutty, *Chronological history*, p. 93; MacArthur, 'Medical history', pp. 265-88; Post, *Food shortage*, pp. 230-1, 233; Geary, 'Famine, fever and the bloody flux', pp. 75-6.

88   Cox to [? Harris], 23 Apr. 1741.

89   Berkeley to [James], [1741]; [Philip Skelton], *The necessity of tillage and granaries in a letter to a member of parliament...* (Dublin, 1741), p. 36.

90   [Skelton], *Tillage and granaries*, pp. 36-7.

91   'Publicola', *A letter from a country gentleman in the province of Munster to his grace the Lord Primate of all Ireland* (n.d., n.p.), p. 3, quoted in Drake, 'Demographic crisis', pp. 103-4.

92   Letter dated 8 July, in [London] *Daily Post*, 1 Aug. 1741.

93   *F.D.J.*, 4-7, 14-18, 25-28 April, 4-7 July, 28 July-1 Aug.1741; [London] *Daily Post*, 21 Apr. 1741; *D.N.L.*, 22-5 Aug. 1741; Jocelyn to Hardwicke, 29 March 1741, in Ball, *Judges*, II, p.131; Burns, *Irish parliamentary politics 1730-1760*, p.53. The Munster circuit was scheduled to begin at Limerick on 4 March and end at Waterford on 6 April: *F.D.J.*, 3-7 Feb. 1740-1.

94   Purcell to Egmont, - Aug. 1741 (B.L. Add. MS 47,006, p.53 [N.L.I. Mic. p4679]); *D.N.L.*, 29 Aug.-1 Sept. 1741; [London] *Daily Post*, 8 Sept. 1741.

95   Jocelyn to Hardwicke, 29 March 1741, in Ball, *Judges*, II, p.131; William Conner, Bandon to Henry Boyle, 5 May 1741 (P.R.O.N.I., Shannon papers, D2707/A/1/4/3).

96   *D.E.P.*, 31 Jan.-3 Feb. 1740-1, 4-7 Apr., 22-25 Aug. 1741; *P.Occ.*, 14-17 Feb. 1740-1; *F.D.J.*, 14-17 March 1740-1, 28-31 March 1741. For a similar story for Kerry (and the very high death rate in Tralee gaol) see *F.D.J.*, 21-4 March 1740-1; Charles Creighton, *A history of epidemics in Britain* (Cambridge, 1894), II, pp. 243-4; and for Kilkenny, *F.D.J.*, 28-31 March 1741. For reports of crime waves in Dublin and in Galway: *F.D.J.*, 31 Jan.-3 Feb., 14-17 Feb. 1740-1.

97   *F.D.J.*, 1-5 Sept. 1741.

98   *F.D.J.*, 7-10, 10-14, 14-17 Feb., 28 Feb.-3 March 1740-1, 24-28 March 1741.

99   Garnham, *Courts, crime and the criminal law*, pp. 161-3.

100   *D.N.L.*, 7-10 March 1740-1; *P.Occ.*, 7-10 March 1740-1, 21-5 Apr. 1741; *D.E.P.*, 7-10 March 1740-1; [London] *Daily Post*, 2 May 1741; *D.N.L.*, 2-6 June 1741.

101   *D.N.L.*, 21-24, 24-28 Feb. 1740-1; 18-21 Apr. 1741. For an attempt to
        storm a food-carrying vessel at Barley Cove in west Cork, see *F.D.J.*,
        10-14 Feb. 1740-1.

102   *F.D.J.*, 8-12 Sept. 1741.

103   *D.N.L.*, 18-22 Aug. 1741; *P.Occ.*, 18-22 Aug. 1741.   A less specific
        municipal proclamation against all vagrants had been published in
        Dublin the previous autumn which seems to have caused little stir:
        F.D.J., 7-11 Oct. 1740.

104   Drake, 'Demographic crisis', p. 121. Note that the foundling deaths-
        to-admission ratio averaged 76% for the five years ending June
        1743.

105   *F.D.J.*, 13-16 June 1741; *D.N.L.*, 1-5, 8-12 Sept. 1741.   188 'miserable
        debtors' had been released in the first two months of 1741, thanks
        to monies raised by the Charitable Music Society: *P.Occ.*, 10-14
        March 1740-1.   A stream of donations to help imprisoned debtors
        get their hands on food was channeled via the *F.D.J.* during the
        spring and summer to the three city debtors' prisons (see for
        example *F.D.J.*, 18-21 April 1741). Cf. David Kelly, 'Insolvents in
        eighteenth-century Dublin', in David Dickson, *The gorgeous mask:
        Dublin 1700-1850* (Dublin, 1987), pp. 98-120.

106   *D.N.L.*, 24-7 Jan. 1740-1; [London] *Daily Post*, 7 Feb. 1740-1.

107   Pearde to Price, 26 March 1741 (Puleston papers); Purcell to
        Egmont, 7 Apr. 1741 (B.L. Add. MSS 47,006, p.23 [N.L.I. Mic.
        p4679]); *F.D.J.*, 2-5 May 1741; *P.Occ.*, 19-23 May 1741; *D.N.L.*, 8-11
        May 1741; Rutty, *Dublin*, II, pp. 356-7.

108   Purcell to Egmont, 1 May 1741; Taylor to Egmont, 29 June 1741
        (Egmont papers, B.L. Add. MS 47,006, pp. 29, 41 [N.L.I. Mic.
        p4679]); Pearde to Price, 12, 24 July, 7 Aug. 1741 (Puleston papers);
        Rutty, *Dublin*, II, p. 468.

109   *D.N.L.*, 30 June-4 July 1741; [London] *Daily Post*, 11 July 1741.

110   [London] *Daily Post*, 1 Aug. 1741.

111   'Plenty: A poem', in Whyte, *Occasional poems*, p.9.

112   *F.D.J.*, 1-4 Aug. 1741.

113   *The distressed state of Ireland considered, more particularly with respect to
        the north...* (n.p., 1740), pp. 4-5.

114   *F.D.J.*, 25-28 Oct. 1740; Thomas M. Truxes, *Irish-American trade
        1660-1783* (Cambridge, 1988), p. 225. The unnamed Mallow author
        reckoned that the 1740 harvest would supply only a quarter of
        domestic grain requirements: [London] *Daily Post*, 5 Nov. 1740.

115   *F.D.J.*, 25-28 Oct. 1740; [London] *Daily Post*, 6 Jan., 7 Feb. 1740-1;
       P.Occ., 13-16 June 1741.

116   All trade statistics are taken from P.R.O.[London], CUST/15. For
       ports of origin see for example *D.N.L.*, 7-11 July 1741. See also
       Truxes, *Irish-American trade*, pp. 224-6.

117   Taylor to Egmont, 11 Sept.; Purcell to Egmont, 6 Oct. 1741 [B.L.
       Add. MS 47,006, pp. 57, 67 [N.L.I. Mic. p4679]); John Usher,
       Lismore, to Sir William Heathcote, 9 Dec. 1741 (Heathcote papers,
       P.R.O.N.I., T. 3091/A3/84); *D.N.L.*, 8-12 Sept. 1741; [London]
       Daily Post, 12, 23 Sept., 1 Oct. 1741; Rutty, *Dublin*, II, p.357. The
       storms do not seem to have such adverse effects in other provinces.

118   Whyte, *Occasional poems... Part the second*, p.2; Brian Boydell, A *Dublin
       musical calendar 1700-60* (Dublin, 1988), pp. 74-86.

119   *Cork Chronicle*, 19 Jan. 1767; T.C.D. MUN/P/23/1485a, petition
       dated 24 June 1784; *Census of Ireland for... 1851, part V, Tables of
       death*, I (Parliamentary papers, 1856, XXIX), p.128; Ignatius Murphy,
       The diocese of Killaloe in the eighteenth century (Dublin, 1991), p.72; [Sir
       Charles Trevelyan], *The Irish crisis* (London, 1847), p.6-7. For a
       nineteenth-century memory of a well's curative powers against the
       dysentery 'about the year 1741-42', see *Ordnance Survey Memoirs of
       Ireland*, XXXVII: *Antrim (Carrickfergus)* (Belfast, 1996), p.8. (I am
       grateful to Peter Carr for drawing my attention to this reference.)

120   Usher to Abdy, 14, 24 Feb. 1740-1, 4 Apr., 16 May 1741 (Lismore
       papers); John Keane and Mathew Hales, Cappoquin to Sir William
       Heathcote, 2 March 1740-1 (Heathcote papers, P.R.O.N.I., T.3091/
       A3/73); Cox to [? Harris], 23 Apr. 1741; Thomas Squire, Kilmacow,
       to Judge Michael Ward, 30 Nov, 1742, (P.R.O.N.I. Ward papers,
       D.2092/1/5/146); Publicola, *Letter*, p.7.

121   *F.D.J.*, 28 July-1 Aug. 1741. The stanza was part of the elegy for
       Archbishop Synge.

122   Data from the Church of Ireland registers are for the most part
       drawn from an ongoing project by the author. Nearly all the
       registers (originals or microfilms) remain unpublished and are
       located in the Representative Church Body Library, Dublin, or in
       the National Archives. But see *The register of the parish of S. Peter and S.
       Kevin 1669-1771* (Dublin, 1911).

123   For Dublin's religious composition at this time, see Dickson, 'The
       demographic implications of Dublin's growth 1650-1850', in R.
       Lawton & R. Lee, eds. *Urban population development in Western Europe...*
       (London, 1989); Patrick Fagan, 'The population of Dublin in the
       eighteenth century', in *Eighteenth-Century Ireland*, vi (1991).

124   Rutty, *Chronological history*, pp. 78-80;   Post, *Food shortage*, pp. 211-2.

125   Rutty, *Chronological history*, p. 85.

126   The greatest volume of burials occurred in May-June 1740 in the Waterford parish, in July-September 1740 in Cork.

127   [London] *Daily Post*, 11 Apr. 1740.

128   *Edward's Cork remembrance* (Cork, 1792), p.150. It is however possible that this refers to the summer of 1741.

129   Little untoward happened until the late autumn of 1740, but burials then crept up over several months to peak in February, March and April 1741. Similar patterns are evident in the register for Youghal, Co. Cork, with a peak in March 1741.

130   William Taylor to the earl of Egmont, 29 June 1741 (Egmont papers, B.L. Add. MS 47,006, p.41 [N.L.I. Mic. p4679]); [London] *Daily Post*, 28 March 1741.

131   *F.D.J.*, 24-28 March, 1-4 Aug., 5-8 Sept. 1741; [London] *Daily Post*, 7 Apr. 1741.

132   Drumglass (Co. Tyrone), Antrim town and Blaris (Co. Antrim). Cf. Glenavy (Co. Antrim) and Templemore (i.e. Derry city).

133   Worthington, 'Death, disease and famine'.

134   [London] *Daily Post*, 1 Sept. 1741. John Post first brought to light this important reference: Post, *Food scarcity*, p. 245. The identity of clergyman in question is not apparent; there must presumably have been a curate in charge under Richard Burgh– who had been rector since 1691: St. John D. Seymour, *The succession of parochial clergy in ...Cashel and Emly* (Dublin, 1908), p. 73.

135   Cox to [?Harris], 23 Apr. 1741; Berkeley to Prior, 19 May 1741.

136   Dickson, O Gráda & Daultrey, 'Hearth tax', 164-8.

137   Squire to Ward, 30 Nov. 1742 (Ward papers); *F.D.J.*, 13-17 Jan. 1740-1; *D.N.L.*, 29 July-2 Aug. 1740; Dickson, O Gráda & Daultrey, 'Hearth tax', 167; Marianne S. Wokeck, 'Irish immigration to the Delaware Valley before the American Revolution', *P.R.I.A.*, xcvii, C (1996), 108, 120, 125. On the swarms of Irish beggars in Cheshire see *F.D.J.*, 23-26 Aug. 1740.

138   'Publicola', *Letter*, pp. 2-3; Thomas P. Power, *Land, politics and society in eighteenth-century Tipperary* (Oxford, 1990), pp. 23-4.

139   For advocacy of this: *D.N.L.*, 25-29 Nov. 1740.

140   [Skelton], *Necessity of tillage*, pp.41-3; *The groans of Ireland...* (Dublin, 1741), pp. 10-7; *A proposal for lessening the excessive price of bread corn in Ireland* (Dublin, 1741); [Thomas Prior] *A proposal to prevent the price of corn from rising too high, or falling too low, by means of granaries* (Dublin, 1741); *A dissertation on the inlargement of tillage, the erecting of public granaries, and the regulating, employing, and supporting the poor of this kingdom* (Dublin, 1741); Caulfield, *Corporation of Cork*, pp.608-9; Howley, *Follies and garden buildings*, pp.211-5.

141   *D.N.L.*, 28 Nov.-1 Dec. 1741; *F.D.J.*, 14-17 Feb. 1740-1; *The Dublin Magazine*, March 1763, p. 148; Alan Browne, ed. *Masters, midwives and ladies-in-waiting: The Rotunda Hospital 1745-1995* (Dublin, 1995), pp. 4-7.

142   Francis H. Tuckey, *The county and city of Cork remembrancer...* (Cork, 1837), p.350; Colman O Mahony, *In the shadows: Life in Cork 1750-1930* (Cork, 1997), pp. 13-5.

143   Burns, *Irish parliamentary politics*, p.54; Garnham, *Courts, crime and the criminal law*, p. 18. The acts are 17 George II, chap. 10 and 17 George II, chap. 5.

144   Dickson, 'In search of the old Irish poor law', pp. 149-59.

145   Post, *Food shortage*, pp. 22, 144-5, 178, 194-5, 225, 269-70.

146   A fuller account of these themes can be found in Dickson, 'The other great Irish famine', in Póirtéir, *Great Irish famine*, pp. 55-9.

Index